THE SILVER LINK L...
RAILWAY MODELLING

●

MORE LAYOUTS FOR
LIMITED SPACES

Despite appearances, Neil Ripley's 'Carlton Metals' layout occupies a space of no more than 4ft 6in long by 1 foot wide (see page 95). *Steve Flint, courtesy of Railway Modeller*

THE SILVER LINK LIBRARY OF RAILWAY MODELLING

●

MORE LAYOUTS FOR LIMITED SPACES

●

Further practical solutions for the space-starved modeller

Nigel Adams

Silver Link Publishing Ltd

First published in 2010

British Library Cataloguing in Publication Data

A catalogue record for this book is available from the British Library.

ISBN 978 1 85794 346 7

Silver Link Publishing Ltd
The Trundle
Ringstead Road
Great Addington
Kettering
Northants NN14 4BW

Tel/Fax: 01536 330588
email: sales@nostalgiacollection.com
Website: www.nostalgiacollection.com

Printed and bound in the Czech Republic

A Silver Link book
from
The NOSTALGIA *Collection*

ACKNOWLEDGEMENTS

I could not have written this book on my own and I particularly want to thank the contributors who have readily written about their layouts and provided photographs and plans. I also want to thank those who have provided prototype photographs. I have been a working volunteer on the Talyllyn Railway for 26 years and thanks are due to the management of the TR for readily letting me use photographs that have been provided, mainly by members, for the railway's use. If the use of these photographs brings a few more passengers to ride on the first preserved railway in the world, it will have been worth it!

Special thanks are due to Sarah Ventry, who typed my text, Doris Southgate, who typed the photo captions, and to Lawrie Bowles, who proof-read the text for me. I am also extremely grateful to my elder son Justin and Ray Reid, who used their computer skills to supplement my very basic computer ability in the production of the manuscript. Justin also helps me with my layouts at exhibitions.

I owe a great debt to Steve Flint, John Emerson and Tony Wright for so readily agreeing to let me use photographs previously used in *Railway Modeller* and *British Railway Modelling* magazines.

Thanks are also due to the members of the Tywyn & District Model Railway Club, of which I was a founder member in November 2001, for their support and friendship. We are only a small club but it is good to meet regularly with like-minded people.

Finally, I have been married to Celia for more than 45 years and she has supported and encouraged me in the hobby all that time. I owe her an immense debt of gratitude for that, and because I have the spare room for my railway modelling and I exhibit at quite a few exhibitions each year, which, because of where we live, often means being away from Friday to Monday. It is to her and my family, Justin, Paul, Clare, Sheryl, Jesse and Matthew, that I dedicate this book.

CONTENTS

A view of most of my 'Frankwell Street Yard' (Mark 2) layout (*above*) and a close-up view of the Mark 1 version. The latter shows scenic detail in the form of two containers, two boilers, a small shed and fuel tanks, both large and small. It also shows how vehicles can be used effectively to add to the scenic detail. *Tony Wright, courtesy of British Railway Modelling/Author*

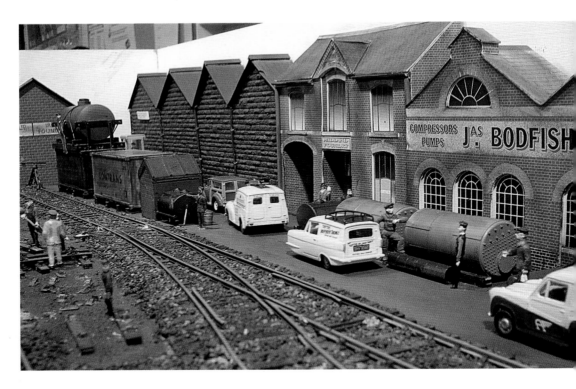

INTRODUCTION

Some 14 years ago I spoke to Will Adams (no relation) and Peter Townsend at Silver Link Publishing Ltd about the possibility of a book. The outcome was my very first book, *Layouts for Limited Spaces*, which was published in September 1996 and, much to my amazement and delight, has been reprinted six times and is still available at the time of writing. This, to my mind, at least shows that there are still plenty of people who, by necessity or choice, want to build a layout in a limited space. It was at the National Model Railway Exhibition at the NEC in November 2008 that the idea for a follow-up book was put to me by Philip Parker. He and I were discussing the fact that my original book was still in print and it included Melbridge Dock, one of Philip's layouts, which he was exhibiting at the NEC that year because it was 20 years since it was first been exhibited at the Warley Show. He suggested that I ask Will and Peter if they thought there was a market for a follow-up book. They and their colleagues said there was – hence this book, *More Layouts for Limited Spaces*. Thanks to Philip for the suggestion, and it is only right that, once again, he is a contributor.

For as long as I have been modelling – now 60 years including my childhood – I have been attracted to small layouts. In retirement Celia and I live in a three-bedroom cottage – thought to have been originally built in the 17th century – so perhaps it is just as well that I like small layouts because I don't have the space for a large one anyway!

I also like building layouts. There is something immensely satisfying in completing a small layout. I know there are those who say 'a layout is never finished', but

you certainly can finish a small layout. Of course, you can change or improve it, maybe by adding extra detail – another facet of our hobby that I enjoy.

Finally, I am one of those modellers who enjoys exhibiting. At present I exhibit at about ten shows a year and organise the Tywyn MRC Exhibition. What I would not want to do is to spend literally hours setting up and dismantling a large layout and driving the necessary 'white van' to and from the exhibition. I have great admiration for the teams of people who do that, but it's just not for me. Small layouts are quicker and easier to set up at shows and my fellow operators and I hope to be on the way home no more than 30 minutes after the exhibition has closed. This is particularly relevant if you live on the west coast of Wales and the exhibition is in the Midlands, for example.

One of the huge advantages of exhibiting your layout is that you meet fellow modellers and, over the years, many of them have become firm friends. Without such friends I would not have been able to write either of my books because they have readily contributed. Such is the camaraderie within the railway modelling fraternity.

Exhibitions are also places where you can learn something new, no matter how long you have been railway modelling. Nobody has the monopoly of

Right: **My 009 MPD, built in 1972, was the first of many layouts of engine sheds I have built, and won the trophy for the best layout for attention to scenic detail at the 1973 Oxford exhibition.** *Brian Wiggins*

good ideas. I know that I am continually learning from fellow modellers and I hope that, in some small way, some of them can learn, or at least get ideas, from my layouts.

Obviously this new book cannot just repeat what was in the first one. Therefore in the first part I have updated that which needed to be updated from the first book because the hobby has 'moved on' since I wrote it, but the basics are still the same.

So this book has a much larger 'SMALL LAYOUTS GALLERY' showing a variety of layouts in various scales and gauges from which I hope the reader will get ideas.

I have also shown some more prototypes suitable for small-space models, and photographs of prototype and model scenic detail, because in my opinion a small layout is ideal for concentrating on scenic detail. That is one of the aspects of modelling that I really enjoy. In 1972 I built an 009 layout of an MPD (see pages 63-65 in *Layouts for Limited Spaces* and the photograph on page 7 of this book). It was only 35 inches by 21 inches, and at the Oxford MRC exhibition in 1973 it received the trophy for the best layout for attention to scenic detail. Ever since then I have found this a particularly fascinating aspect of our hobby.

For the benefit of those who have not yet read *Layouts for Limited Spaces* (published in a

larger format and still available from Silver Lin Publishing) here is a summary of what was covered besides the 'Small layouts gallery' (which contained details of 30 layouts in various scales and gauges)

- Why build small layouts?
- What is a small layout?
- Types of small layout
- Where put a small layout
- Prototype ideas
- Stations
- Loco sheds and works
- Designing small layouts
- Portability
- Planning
- Fiddle yards
- Layout supports
- Electrics and point control
- Scenery
- Rolling stock and operation
- Rolling stock
- Operating methods
- Compiling a sequence of operations
- Preparing for exhibition
- The ultimate: a room of its own for your layout

This book, then, is effectively 'Volume 2'.

A scene on a previous 'engine shed' layout built my me in the late 1990s. *Author*

1
WHERE CAN I GET SOME IDEAS?

So you have decided to build a small (compact) layout, but you are not sure what to build and you are looking for ideas. Where do you start looking?

The most obvious place is the model railway press. In this country we are blessed with very good monthly magazines and they regularly feature small or compact layouts. This is hardly surprising because many of us live in small houses or flats where the demands of our family mean that there is not the luxury of a spare room that can be used solely as the 'model railway room'.

This is perhaps more true now than when I wrote *Layouts for Limited Spaces* because the price of property (even allowing for the 2008 'slump') is such that many young people cannot afford to move out of the parental home to get on the property ladder.

Also, there are people who do have the space or spare room to build a larger layout, but choose not to do so for various reasons. It may be that husband and wife choose to share a 'hobbies room', which at least means they are not separated for hours at a time while pursuing their respective interests and hobbies.

It may be that the modeller has, like me and many others, deliberately chosen to build a small, easily transportable layout so that it can be taken to exhibitions and be quickly set up and dismantled. Such layouts are also attractive to exhibition managers who want to keep a balance between large layouts and ones that people can easily accommodate at home.

Smaller layouts are also attractive to exhibition managers because they are cheaper! What I mean by this in that a small layout can usually be accommodated in the average family car together with the rolling stock and necessary 'paraphernalia' and the operators (ie driver and passenger).

This leads naturally to the second place where you can look for ideas – exhibitions! Whether the exhibition is a large one such as the Warley Show at the NEC or a small local show, the organiser(s) will try to have a good cross-section of layouts. In my opinion it is particularly important to do this because, if 'Mr and Mrs Average' bring their children along and only see large layouts, they might conclude that railway modelling is not for them. That would be a disaster because, as with every hobby or sport, we need new blood if it is to continue.

From my own experience of exhibiting small layouts I am sure that they will continue to be built, both out of necessity and choice, and this is confirmed by the conversations I have had with exhibition visitors of all ages.

The publisher of *British Railway Modelling* (Warners Group Publications plc) produces a series of books covering various aspects of the hobby. Book 5 is particularly relevant to the subject of this book. It was published in October 2008 and is entitled 'Model Railways the easy way – a practical guide to making compact layouts for the railway modeller'. It was written and photographed by Peter Marriott (a prolific writer for model railway magazines), with one chapter entitled 'Next Steps' written by Ian Futers. Ian is well known for producing high-class compact layouts, currently in 7mm scale but in smaller scales before that.

Another factor that encourages small transportable layouts is the design and size of present-day cars. I worked in the car industry from 1958 to 1986 before training for ordination and I saw the transformation from family saloons and estate cars to hatchbacks and three- and five-door saloons with fold-down seats. Since I left the car industry 24 years ago this has become more noticeable, so that now even the smallest cars have a hatchback and folding seats.

This is particularly attractive as we seek to improve our carbon footprint. For example, the road-fund tax on a Citroen C1 or Peugeot 107 is now only £35! This compares with £150 for my previous car (a Citroen Berlingo). Other examples

of small family cars are the Hyundai I10, Citroen C2, Skoda Fabia and Chevrolet Matiz.

To illustrate the possible space available in such cars, I have ascertained that the Hyundai I10 has a space measuring 40 inches between the wheel arches and 40 inches from the rear of the front seats to the tailgate. This I remember is similar to the space available in the rear of a Metro, of which I had a number when I worked in the car industry. My current car a Skoda Fabia has 50 inches from the rear of the front seats to the tailgate with 37 inches between the wheel arches and 48 inches between

the rear doors. The only way to ensure that your layout fits into your car is to carefully measure both the car and the layout!

Also, do not forget to allow space for the stock box, tool box, controllers, lighting, etc. Of course the lighting and the controller can be built into the layout, and this saves space.

If your layout is long and thin you can transport it by folding one half (or one third, depending on the car design) of the rear seat and reclining the front passenger seat. I have done this with more than one layout. As long as the dimensions of the folded layout are no more than about 66 inches by 15 inches it will work. Again, check the dimensions carefully first!

Either way, you can transport your layout associated equipment and two operators easily in a small family car. If space is really at a premium you can fold the layout in half as we do with one of our club layouts – Common Lane Wharf. When set up the layout measures 4 feet by 2 feet, but when folded for transport it is only 2 feet by 2 feet and 16 inches high. The folding of the layout also means that the buildings and scenery do not get damaged in transit.

When transporting my small layouts, I crate the two scenic boards face to face by bolting them through plywood ends to separate them, and also bolting on a front protecting piece of plywood. If the layout is small and in one piece, I fit a 'lid' that is either bolted on or held in place with over-centre catches.

Above left: **Common Lane Wharf is a small folding layout built by the late Mike Pearson and Steve Best of Hull MRS and subsequently bought by the Tywyn MRC. The layout consists of two solid-top baseboards that are hinged. When closed, two struts are bolted to the outside ends, and this makes a very compact 'crate' for storage and transport and protects the scenery and track.** *Neil Ripley*

Left: **Myself (right) and Bob Worthington with Common Lane Wharf at the Porthmadog Exhibition in 2008.** *Nigel Hughes, Porthmadog*

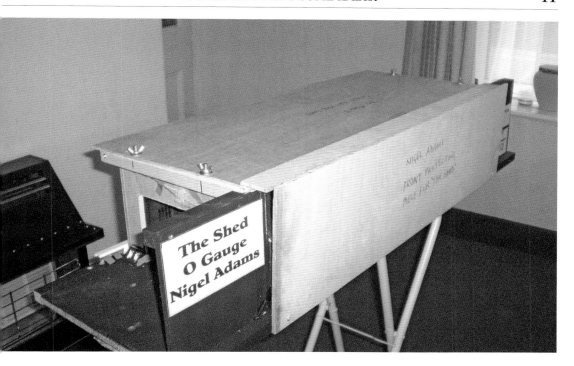

Above: 'The Shed' ready to go to an exhibition. The top is bolted on with four bolts and the front is fixed with three screws. It no longer stands on the ironing board at shows but on the framework shown in the photograph on page 38, which allows a shelf behind the layout for storing locos, etc. *Author*

Below: One of my previous layouts had L-shaped protection, held in place by four over-centre catches. The layout was stored like this in a shed as well as transported to and from shows. *Author*

2
WHERE CAN I BUILD A LAYOUT WHERE I LIVE?

The flippant answer to this question is that it depends on what sort of house you live in! But, to be serious, if you want to be able to operate the layout in situ then it is obvious that it must be permanently erected somewhere unless it is so small that it can be brought out of a cupboard and quickly set up. A number of people have built layouts in box files, and one such layout by Phil Parker is described in Chapter 9. Another example of a 'box layout' is Southon Yard, which was described in the June 2007 *Railway Modeller*; it was built by Michael Campbell in 009 scale in a shoe box.

If the layout is to be permanently erected, various possibilities come to mind. In the living room it could be built along one or two walls, but it is important to make the layout and whatever it is supported on (cupboards or bookshelves, for example) look tidy and presentable.

A bedroom or a spare room is another possibility. My son Justin has done this in the 'box room' in his house, and the accompanying plan shows how he has accommodated his layout bench and storage. This is 'utopia', because you can have your workbench here and store model railway equipment under the layout. I also do this. My latest layout is supported on cheap shelving from Ikea and my wife made curtains that cover the shelves and make the area look tidy. My layout and my work bench take up one wall of our smallest

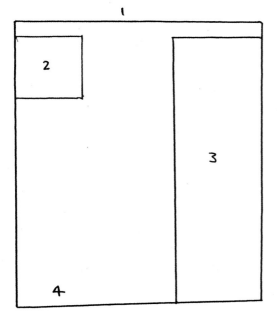

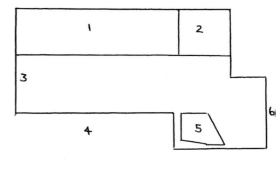

Left: **A sketch of Justin's modelling room (not to scale). 1 Window, 2 Workbench, 3 Layout on top of old kitchen unit used for storage, 4 Door**

Above: **My modelling room (not to scale). 1 Layout on top of Ikea shelves, 2 Bench, 3 Door, 4 Staircase, 5 Desk, 6 Window**

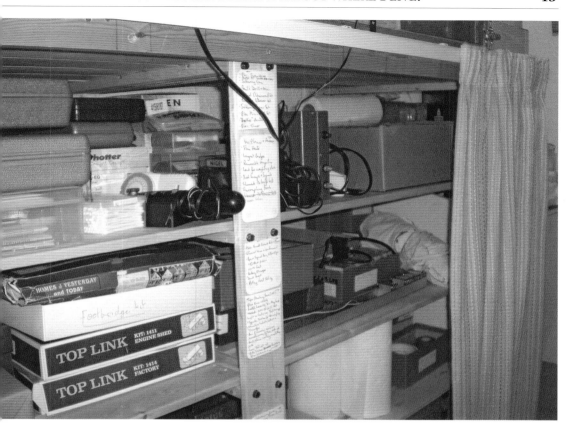

The Ikea shelving under my layout in the spare room: curtains cover it and the cards pinned to the upright show what is stored and where. *Author*

bedroom and, because the room is L-shaped, I am also able to accommodate my computer work station/desk too.

Other possibilities are an alcove or alcoves; an under-stairs cupboard; along a landing; or in the loft, if it is easily accessible and the design allows for sufficient headroom. A layout could either be permanently erected or hinged to fold up against a wall in a garage or garden shed; as long as the building is properly insulated and heated this has a lot to commend it. I have done it twice. Getting the electricity to the shed is obviously vitally important – consult an electrician.

If the layout is not to be permanently erected at home, storage options come readily to mind. My elder son Justin and I stored our layouts on end in a built-in wardrobe in one of the vicarages I lived in. You could also store the layout together with all your equipment in an old wardrobe.

Alternatively you could erect racking in the garage or shed. I currently have an 8 feet by 6 feet shed in the garden in which I have built wooden racks using chipboard and 2-by-1-inch timber. This provides me with shelves on which I can store three small layouts, spare timber and other associated model railway equipment. I still have room for a bench and shelves on either side of the window on the other wall as well as two cheap bookshelves no longer needed in the house.

Some people simply crate the layout and stand the crate in the garage or shed. I have done this once, and it greatly helps in moving the layout if the bottom of the crated layout rests on a piece of timber to which are fixed four castors. In this way, lifting is reduced to a minimum.

Some 30 years ago a fellow Talyllyn Railway volunteer, Malcolm Clarke, built a superb 4mm-scale narrow-gauge layout called 'The Gwynedd Railway'. It was described in the 1979 issue of

Above: **My 8 feet by 6 feet shed in the garden. There is** **small workbench under the window.** *Author*

Left: **The inside of the shed has been lined with 'gre** **insulation and simple racking made on which to sto** **layouts, etc. The top shelf is for timber 'bits and pieces'. Tl** **layouts seen stored are 'The Shed' and its associated boxe** **and a Gn15 layout.** *Author*

Railway Modeller and is also included here in Chapte 9. The baseboards were made of half-inch chipboar on 2-by-1-inch framing, and the chipboard was cu away where the scenery fell below baseboard leve this ensured maximum rigidity. No doubt toda Malcolm would probably use plywood for lightnes The framework and the baseboard were glued an screwed. The boards measured 36 by 18 inches an were arranged in two stacks of three for transpo and storage. The uppermost of the three boards wa supported on four 2-by-1-inch legs braced togeth at the centre and the bottom with horizontal 2 by-1-inch runners, which formed the runners ont which the other two boards in the stack slid. Th overall dimension of the three stacked boards was 36 inches by 22 inches by 36 inches high. The extra 4-inch width enabled storage sidings to be carried at the back of the top board on one stack and the control panel on the other stack.

If you wanted to follow this idea you could add plywood round the stack for protection of the boards, perhaps also with a plywood top. Doing this would not add much weight but would give total protection to the layout if it was stored in a garage or a shed, and certainly in transit to and from exhibitions.

A third alternative is to build an extension or a conservatory, but that would be very expensive!

Finally, there is what some people might call a 'gimmicky layout'. By this I mean a layout in a coffee table or in a glass-fronted case to make a 'working diorama'. I personally think that these have a lot to commend them, and in fact I am associated with two such layouts.

The TRPS is the owner of a superb diorama layout of Dolgoch Falls, which is described in Chapter 9, and the Tywyn MRC is building an OO loco depot layout in a coffee table that we bought second-hand for £5! This too has castors on the legs for ease of movement. The layout is on the bottom level and we have fitted interior lighting

under the top. At shows and in the clubroom it rests on trestles bought from Aldi for £9.99 each, which are superb value.

Some people have built layouts in a chest of drawers. An example by Chris Lawton was featured

Above: **Under the bottom shelf a layout under construction is stored on a piece of 12mm plywood fitted with castors so that it can be easily moved. When the layout is finished it will still be stored there, but with a protective top and front.** *Author*

Below: **Malcolm Clarke's method of storing and crating for transport his Gwynedd Railway layout.**

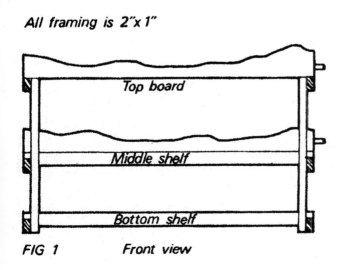

All framing is 2″x 1″

Top board

Middle shelf

Bottom shelf

FIG 1   **Front view**

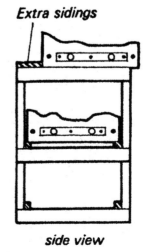

Extra sidings

side view

in the September 2001 *Railway Modeller* and there have been others.

These are just a few ideas – there is no limit to people's ingenuity. Small layouts in various home locations are regularly described in the model railway press and many can be seen at exhibitions up and down the country. I have built three layouts on ironing boards over the years and my latest is described in Chapter 9.

Model Railway Journal No 100, published in 1998, describes a superb 7mm layout – 'St George Hill' – which fits into the case of a grandfather clock. It has appeared at many exhibitions and it is well worth trying to find a copy of that issue just to read about this really ingenious layout.

Model Railroader magazine publishes various small books about small layouts; they are available in the UK and you can get some good ideas from them. That does not mean that you have to build an American layout, although, of course, you can if you wish.

Just a part of the huge O-gauge layout I visited in Texas in 2004. Look at all the space for pictures! *Author*

One possible location I have not mentioned is the basement, commonly used by our American friends, but they are so huge that they really fall outside the scope of this book. On a visit to the USA in 2004 I met a modeller with a huge basement that was absolutely full of a superb 7mm layout; but I have to say that he bought the plot so that the basement room could be large, and designed the house to fit on top! Just to make you envious I include a couple of photographs. (*Opposite and left*)

Left: The owner of this huge layout in the sitting area of the basement, which also has a 'dirty room', a workspace, a toilet and a fridge! Just the opposite of a limited space! *Author*

Below: Bob Hey and myself at Guildex 2005 with 'Dolgoch' (see Chapter 9). This is ingeniously constructed to be transported in two parts and was well ahead of its time when it was designed more than 50 years ago. *Justin Adams*

3
MORE PROTOTYPE IDEAS

The prototypes you may wish to look at will depend on where your interests lie. For example, I like building small layouts of locomotive depots. This is partly because it saves a lot of bother coupling and uncoupling, but mainly because I have nearly 40 locomotives in O gauge and 12 in Gn15 scale. Therefore I am not particularly interested in looking at plans of stations.

Alternatively, if you're interested in shunting and you like building wagons, you are going to be attracted to small goods yards or sidings. You may also be attracted to small stations where there is a mix of passenger and goods operation.

The prototype plan you might consider will also be affected by what scale you choose to model in. It is obvious that someone modelling in N gauge can get far more in a given space than someone who models in O gauge. Also, whether you model steam or modern image, or standard or narrow gauge, will affect what prototype ideas you look at.

All this may seem to be stating the blindingly obvious, but there are some people who want to take up railway modelling and have a number of interests. Therefore they need to choose which one to follow as far as modelling is concerned.

Finally, there are some people for whom faithfully modelling a specific prototype is what they really want to do. The choice is yours.

Once you know what you want to model you can have a lot of fun looking at various prototype ideas, either on site if possible, or by seeking information from books, photographs or the internet. One very important point if you are able to visit your chosen prototype is that it is essential to ask someone in authority before you start wandering around taking photographs and measuring up. I am a volunteer on the Talyllyn Railway and often act as the Duty Controller; although the majority of enquirers do ask permission, we are finding an increasing number of people who seem to think that they can just step off the platform and cross the line to take photographs. A recent 'classic' was someone who decided to walk up the line from Wharf to the Works at Pendre because he wanted to photograph a particular engine! Apart from the fact that he was technically trespassing, he was totally unaware of shunting movements at Pendre, and could have been injured.

Peter Kazer has built some superb models of narrow gauge prototypes, and brought his model of Corris to one of the Tywyn MRC exhibitions. It certainly drew the visitors and the prototype is not far from where I live – albeit much of it now gone. But Peter investigated the history and produced this wonderful model see the photograph (on page 21).

Living where I do in Tywyn, obviously narrow gauge prototypes are easy to find; 4mm-scale models have been made of Wharf Station and 7mm models of other parts of the TR – Bob Hailes's 'Talyllyn Country' springs to mind. Quarry Siding or Brynglas loops would make good models, and I know that Abergynolwyn has been modelled. If you want a small terminus 'on a shelf' with plenty of height and three distinct levels Nant Gwernol would make a good prototype.

If you prefer a modern prototype, Machynlleth Diesel Depot would be a good one to model. The rock face behind it provides an unusual feature. As I have already said, I am keen on layouts of engine sheds generally – steam or diesel.

If you want to model something different, the Fairbourne Railway offers a lot of scope, perhaps in Gn15.

If you like modelling canals and canal boats a good example is in Peter Marriott's BRM book.

Opposite top: **Wharf station in the rain! Loco No 1** *Talyllyn* **heads two of the original coaches and the original brake-van – 1865 stock running in the 21st century!** *TR collection*

Opposite bottom: **An old picture of the water tower at Wharf. It is very different today and I doubt if it would be allowed under Health & Safety rules! I love the way the tank is tipped towards the loco.** *David Mitchell*

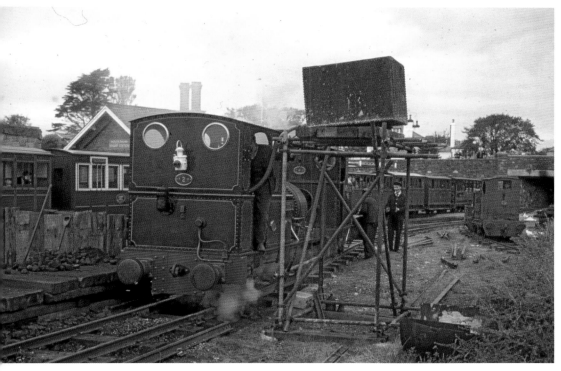

Left and below: Less than 100 yards from home. These two views of Pendre on the Talyllyn Railway are looking east and west respectively. This is another superb location to model and, if you ask, you will be allowed to take all the photographs you need – but please do ask as there are many loco and train movements in the yard that are not timetabled. *Both T collection*

Right: Another prototype not far from home for me. This is the Corris Railway with its new loco outside Maespoeth Shed. Note, too, the 'clutter' to the right of the loco so typical of such scenes and so easily modelled. *David Mitchell*

Above: Prototype inspiration and absolutely superb modelling! Peter Kazer and his layout 'Corris' at Tywyn MRC Exhibition. *Erfyl Lloyd Davis Photography*

Below: Bob Hailes's superb layout 'Talyllyn Country' was on the exhibition circuit for a number of years. The station in the photograph is Rhydyronen. *Bob Hailes*

Left: An engineering train and a passenger train cross at Quarry Siding. Because the track is 'on a shelf' here it would make a good model – road at ground level, track on the 'shelf' and hills above. *TR collection*

Below: No 1 Talyllyn comes into Brynglas loop in the down direction with the block post (signal box) on the left. The train consists of two of the original coaches, the original brake-van and two slate wagons. *TR collection*

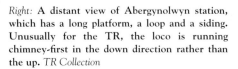

Right: A distant view of Abergynolwyn station, which has a long platform, a loop and a siding. Unusually for the TR, the loco is running chimney-first in the down direction rather than the up. *TR Collection*

Left: **A distant view of No 2 Dolgoch and a vintage train at Nant Gwernol station. This too has a loop and a siding. Originally this was where the slate wagons came down the incline from the quarry at Bryn Eglwys. The incline to the village (superbly modelled in the past by Gordon Gravett) is out of the picture to the right. I think this station has distinct modelling possibilities!** *TR Collection*

Below: **The Isle of Man Railway is another superb prototype (see Robin Winter's layout 'Port Foxdale' in Chapter 9).** *David Mitchell*

Right: **Sadly Ventnor station on the Isle of Wight is long since closed, but the Isle of Wight Steam Railway is well worth a visit in its preserved state. Ventnor station would be ideal for the space-starved modeller as the line disappeared into a tunnel almost immediately.** *David Mitchell*

entitled *Model Railways The Easy Way*, pages 24-27; the layout is called 'Peats Wharf'.

So, the message is 'decide what you want to model' and look for ideas from the prototype you have chosen. Of course, you do not have to follow the prototype exactly unless you want to. There are many layouts to be seen at exhibitions that are excellent but do not model a particular prototype. In fact, I would go so far to say that the majority of model railways fall into that category.

Unfortunately there are some people who 'look down their noses' at layouts that do not slavishly follow the prototype. However, our hobby is a 'broad church' and there is room for everyone. Never forget – it is your layout and what you say goes! I was once exhibiting at Derby and saw a sign on a layout that I have copied and display on my layouts at exhibitions. It is entitled 'Rules of the Layout' and reads as follows:

1.   This is my layout.
2.   Discussions are welcome.
3.   In the event of possible perceived inaccuracies or operational errors, re-read Rule 1!

Above and below: **Something completely different, but on** **14 miles from home. These two views show the new dep** **at Machynlleth station operated by Arriva Trains (Wale** **Ltd.** *Both Author*

It often causes some amusement and a lot of people say that they agree with it wholeheartedly. Interestingly, no one has ever taken me to task over it, but that probably means that they just pass by! That is their choice, and I respect it.

Factory sidings provide good prototype locations for small layouts, such as those at Morris Cowley, Swindon and Longbridge in the car industry, in which I used to work. (In fact, I negotiated the contract for British Rail to move Allegro pressings from Swindon to Longbridge.) Neil Ripley has a very good plan for a layout based on Longbridge sidings in the book *Model Railway Planning and Design Handbook* (Santona Publications), which is full of excellent layout plans and actual layouts designed and built by first-class modellers who regularly show their layouts at exhibitions up and down the country. The possibilities are endless, especially when combined

with the modeller's own imagination.

Another prolific modeller of small layouts usually with a Scottish flavour, although not alway – is Ian Futers. Ian regularly exhibits his layouts an has also written a book for Santona Publicatior entitled *Modelling Scotland's Railways*, which is als full of ideas and prototypes. A more recent Santon Publications book is *Building Micro Layouts* by Pa

unn, an absolute goldmine for people with very little space.

My son Justin built a layout called 'Mullacombe', which included a timber yard, another good prototype to model. In Volume 2 of the Gauge 0 Guild book *Small Layouts* there is an excellent layout based on a small brickworks in 7mm scale (14mm gauge), which measures only 36 by 20 inches. It is simply called 'The Brickworks' and its builder is Arthur Budd.

In the August 2007 issue of *British Railway Modelling (BRM)* there was a very good 3mm layout called 'Fourtee Colliery' by Doug Richards, and in the November 1999 issue there was a lovely N-gauge layout based on Masham (see Chapter 4).

above: A scene from the past that is being modelled by a current TR volunteer: this is Penmaenpool shed on the long-closed Dolgellau to Barmouth line. It is now a superb walk and cycle track and was featured in Julia Bradbury's *Railway Walks* series on BBC TV. Don't miss it if you are in the area! *David Mitchell*

Right: Twelve miles from Tywyn the Fairbourne Railway, and this is Fairbourne station. This, too, has distinct modelling possibilities, especially as the Cambrian Coast line runs past over a road crossing at right angles to the end of the station area. *Author*

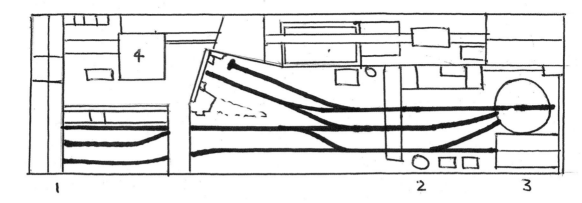

Above: **A plan of 'Fourtee Colliery' by Doug Richards (3ft 4in by 1 foot). 1 Coal drops, 2 Water tank, 3 Engine shed, 4 Colliery buildings over sector plate and storage roads**

If you go to exhibitions, have a look at the surplus magazine stands. For next to nothing you can usually pick up second-hand copies that contain excellent layout ideas that you can either copy or use as the basis of an idea. Remember, after all the years people have been modelling railways, there can be very few really original ideas left. In any case, imitation is a form of flattery!

Because magazines take up such a lot of space to store, for some years I have cut out articles I wish to keep and put them in lever arch files (I now have three full ones); the discarded parts of the magazines are then recycled. Here are just a few examples from my collection:

'Neptune Street Yard' (*Railway Modeller,* Feb 2008)

'Belmont Road' (*Railway Modeller,* Aug 2008)

'George Street Stabling Point' (*Railway Modeller,* May 2007)

'Anywhere TMD' (*Hornby Magazine,* Dec 2008)

'Trainspotters Delight' (*British Railway Modelling,* Apr 1997)

'Four by one' ('Trawden') (*Railway Modeller,* Dec 1990)

This last layout is by Neil Rushby, who is a contributor to this book, and is one of many small layouts he has built over the years.

Below: **A plan of 'Trawden' by Neil Rushby (4 feet by 1 foot). 1 Sector plate, 2 Mill, 3 Goods yard, 4 Level crossing, 5 Station building, 6 Timber yard**

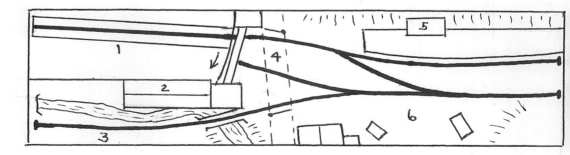

4
DESIGNING SMALL LAYOUTS

In December 1997 Neil Rushby wrote an article in *British Railway Modelling* entitled 'Planning for Realism'. Neil could be described as a 'blunt Yorkshireman' and in the article he says that unoriginality and lack of realism seems to stem from copying layouts and themes rather than going out and finding inspiration first-hand'. He goes on to say, 'Get out there and get looking for yourself.' Neil practices what he preaches and has been kind enough to contribute to the '**SMALL LAYOUTS GALLERY**' in this book with one of his layouts.

In 1997 he was living in York and found three good ideas for layouts within easy travelling distance of home. First was the railway workshops in York, comprising carriage works and the lesser-known wagon repair shops. Neil realised that the south end of the wagon repair shops was 'a very modellable proposition, being compact and simple with a potentially interesting operating problem'. The workshops could be easily made using the Dapol Engine Shed kit, probably with a new roof. The Dapol station building kit would make an

ideal mess room, the pipe bridge could be made from the Dapol signal gantry kit and Dapol railway workmen could populate the layout.

There is an ample supply of wagons – proprietary and kit-built – and, because a wagon repair works was being modelled, they could be a mixture of ex-works and weathered finishes. There are also a number of suitable locos on the market – steam or diesel – and the increasing range of road vehicles now available gives you plenty of choice.

In the same article Neil produced a plan for a layout based on Damems on the Keighley & Worth Valley Railway, and one for a layout based on Marsden – the last stop before Standedge Tunnel on the LNWR route to Manchester. It is a very much compressed version of the station, but leaves space for its magnificent setting.

A fantastic layout – now at the Midland Railway Trust HQ at Butterley – is 'Elmwell Village Depot', designed and built by Brian Jenkins. It is, in fact, four layouts in one. The track plan is identical for each layout, but each depicts a different scene: 'Spring in the 1900s', 'Summer in the 1920s', 'Autumn in the late 1930s', and 'Winter in the early 1950s.' Each layout measures 72 by 16 inches,

Below: **Neil Rushby's 'York Wagonworks'.** *Courtesy of* **BRM**

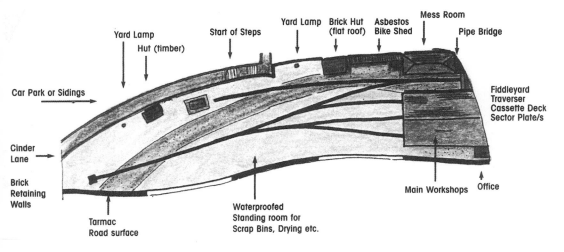

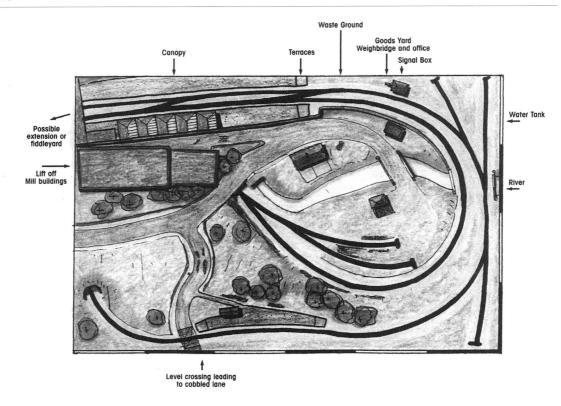

and Brian ingeniously made the boards from two lightweight doors made from very thin veneer sheets bonded together with a cardboard 'eggshell' piece between them. The doors were reduced to a length of 72 inches (from 80 inches) and a 1¼-inch slot was cut in the centre of each door (see the accompanying plan); they were then slotted together at right angles as shown, with two squares

Neil Rushby's 'Damems' (above) and 'Marsden' (below)
Courtesy of BRM

of quarter-inch plywood as end boards to hold them square. It was all bonded together using glass-fibre tape and resin. The whole thing then became a rotating assembly and there was a sector plate at each end. To add to the realism, a Q kits sound system was incorporated into the layout.

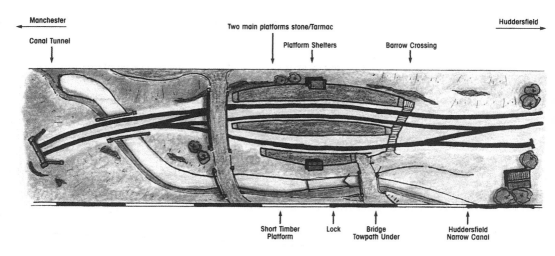

The main disadvantage of the layout was that it needed a Transit-type van to transport it to and from exhibitions. However, the basic idea was first class and you could have four different yet identical layouts – with stock to match – stacked on a rack in the shed or the garage and use or exhibit whichever one you chose.

Earlier I said that I like building models of loco sheds. I am not alone in this and a very good example of such a layout is 'Eastbridge MPD' built by Bob London of East Grinstead MRC and described in the December 1998 issue of *BRM*. It is built on two boards, and a third board contains the fiddle yard, giving a total length of 10ft 6in. The layout is partly based on Redhill; there is a three-road engine shed, a coaling stage, a water tower and a turntable. Locos arrive on shed and are coaled, watered, turned if required, then tabled. Coal wagons supply the coaling stage.

Above: **A tram loco arrives with a mixed train and passes the shops.** *Tony Wright, courtesy of BRM*

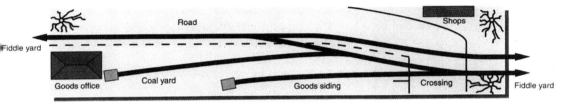

Above: **The track plan for all four of the 'Elmwell' layouts.** *Courtesy of BRM*

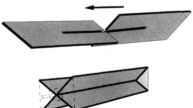

Above: **Brian Jenkins's ingenious method of creating four baseboards in a single unit.** **Courtesy of** *BRM*

Left: **'Elmwell Village':** a Sentinel loco arrives in the yard while the gang takes a break. **Tony Wright,** *courtesy of BRM*

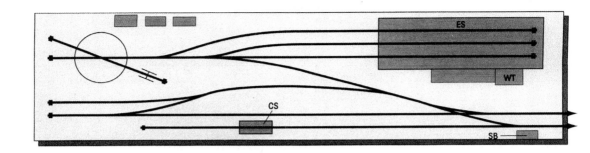

Above: **'Eastbridge MPD', by Bob London of East Grinstead MRC.** *Courtesy of BRM*

Another engine shed layout is Alistair George's 'Swansea Riverside'. This is built on two main boards 1200 by 500mm tapering to 400mm where they join in the centre, with a 40 by 25mm fiddle yard cantilevered off the left-hand board. The smallness of the layout means that two three-way points are used, because they save a vast amount of space. I think this is a superb 7mm layout and one that could be easily stored and transported face-to-face.

Earlier I referred to Neil Rushby's plan for a layout based on the wagon repair works at York. Keith Wright built such a layout called 'Cripple Corner'; I have seen it a number of times at exhibitions and it really has atmosphere. Because

it had to fit in a small hatchback car, the size of the layout was restricted to 6 feet by 1ft 6in, constructed of two 3 feet by 1ft 6in boards. In my opinion the scenery is particularly effective. The layout is set in the North East of England in the mid-1980s in an industrialised area, which allowed Keith to use buildings and walls at the back and ends of the layout. The wagon works is lit and there are also various yard lamps. The layout uses modern rolling stock.

When writing about his layout in the Winter 2004 issue of *Modern Railway Modelling*, Keith wrote, '...if you need to justify the reason why you should build exhibition layouts, then this is why. To encourage more people to do so, to share your ideas, which will keep the hobby alive and bring in more new/young modellers' – an admirable philosophy with which I entirely agree.

Below: **Alistair George's 'Swansea Riverside'.** *Courtesy of BRM © Dan Wilson, Pacific Studio*

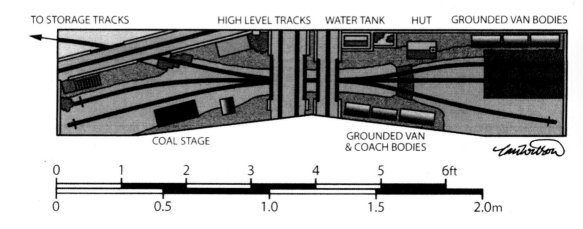

TO STORAGE TRACKS   HIGH LEVEL TRACKS   WATER TANK   HUT   GROUNDED VAN BODIES

COAL STAGE

GROUNDED VAN & COACH BODIES

0   1   2   3   4   5   6ft

0   0.5   1.0   1.5   2.0m

Don't forget that there is a prototype for everything, and I have a photo to prove it – No 6079 on a proving run on the Cambrian Coast line a few years ago, before being used on the summer steam specials. The photograph shows No 76079 at Tywyn with just one coach. So if you have a small layout and want a 'largish' loco and one coach to run on it, here is the prototype.

Also, by coincidence, in 2005 we were on holiday in Whitby and the same loco was being used to connect with the North Yorkshire Moors Railway. The purpose of showing this photograph is to point out that it is perfectly possible to have a steam loco running on your layout with a very

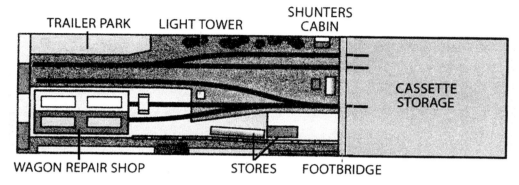

Above: **Keith Wright's 'Cripple Corner'.** *Courtesy of BRM*

Below: **An overall view of 'Cripple Corner', a superb layout in a small space.** *Tony Wright, courtesy of BRM*

Above: Real atmosphere! A very convincing night scene on 'Cripple Corner'. *Tony Wright, courtesy of BRM*

Left: My layout in the spare room is operated from the front. The box at the end once held cheese and a bottle of port, but now holds small transformers to power the lighting and other scenic effects on the layout. *Author*

ight: **A prototype for everything! A tender
…co and one coach are seen at Tywyn, on a
…st run on the Cambrian Coast before the
…ummer steam specials.** *Author*

…elow: **No 76079 is seen again at Whitby,
…his time with a longer train. The new Co-
…p store on former railway land behind
…e wall shows that you can 'update' your
…cation.** *Author*

…odern building nearby. I do not know what stood …ehind the brick wall in the photograph before it was …emolished and replaced by a Co-op supermarket. …his is also true of Tywyn, where the Co-op built a …upermarket on what was the goods yard.

Also, don't forget that layouts can be operated …om the front. The vast majority of layouts at …xhibitions are operated from behind, but if you …perate the layout at home you won't see much …f it if the viewing side is always up against the …all of the room. I have built two layouts that were …perated from the front, and my layout in the spare room is another, so that both myself and the visitors can always see the layout rather than having to peer over the top of the backscene. Operating from the front at shows has two advantages. The public can see what you are doing, and that is good because, when operating from the rear of the layout, people often ask if they can have a look at the controls. Secondly, you are nearer the public and can easily talk to them, which also seems to be appreciated.

The accompanying photos show my first 'Frankwell Street Yard' layout with my elder son, Justin, operating at the CovGOG 2005 Exhibition.

You can see from the first one that the cassette area is also easily viewable, as are the cards with the operating sequence written on them. The other photo shows a more close-up view of virtually the whole layout, again showing the operating sequence cards at the top right-hand side.

Lastly, if you see a clever idea at a show and you want to record it for possible future use, you can always ask if you can take a photograph or two if you have taken a digital camera. But please, **always ask!** It is not only good manners but you should remember that people who suffer from epilepsy can be adversely affected by flashlight.

The next photos were taken at the Gauge O Guild Telford Show a few years ago and show very clearly how the sector plates at either end of the layout cleverly feed the storage sidings behind it.

For those who have internet access the website www.carendt.com covers small layouts – what they call 'micro layouts' – and although some are very small indeed, there are a lot of good ideas. The site is updated at least monthly with new examples and ideas, so is well worth a look. Carl Arendt has also written two books – *Creating Micro Layouts and Carl Arendt's Small Layout Scrapbook* – which, although published in the USA, are available in this country; I bought mine at exhibitions.

Layouts that have to be stored need to be light, which also helps if the layout is to be exhibited. As the basis for their layouts our American friends often use 2-inch 'pink insulation' – if I can call it that – sometimes using two layers to make it 4 inches thick. This has the advantage of being easily carved for scenic purposes, but you cannot very easily bring the wiring underneath for obvious reasons, unless you 'frame' the insulation with plywood – say 6 inches deep. I think it is advisable to do this anyway for protection of the insulation..

You can also use foamboard, which can be obtained from artists' shops or sometimes free from supermarkets and big retailers because they use it for signs. A framework can be made up using a hot glue gun to hold the parts together. Again, I think

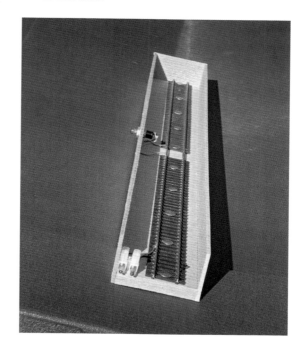

Above and below: Two views of cassettes built by Justin for his new layout. Note that the track is simply proprietary track held in position by drawing pins, which is surprisingly effective. The cassettes are made of MDF and the one shown is split into two electrical sections, hence the push-to-make switch. *Both author*

Left: 'Frankwell Street Yard" (Mark 3) is seen at the CovGOG exhibition in Coventry being operated from the front by my elder son, Justin. Note the cassette area in the foreground and the operating sequence cards by Justin's hand in the first picture and in the top right-hand corner of the second. *Both author*

it is advisable to frame it with plywood to protect it, and it is certainly necessary to use wood at the ends if you are bolting boards together.

One way of saving space when designing a small layout is to use cassettes in the hidden sidings, which I have done on a number of occasions. I have found that the simplest way is to use proprietary track pinned or screwed to a plywood or MDF base with plywood or hardboard sides. Pieces of plywood or thick Plasticard or card can be slotted into the ends to avoid any rolling stock falling out when the cassettes are moved. Connection to the track on the main layout is obviously required, and the easiest method is to use 'choc strip' plugs and sockets; these have the added advantage of locating the cassette so that the tracks line up. Another method is to use aluminium angle screwed to the base and to make the electrical contact with bulldog clips. This also enables you to align the tracks as well as make electrical contact.

Another method widely used by modeller

Left: **A cassette on my O-gauge layout 'Frankwell Street Yard'. As with Justin's layout, connection to the track on the main baseboard is via the 'choc strip' with pins. This is very simple and effective and the idea came from a friend (Steve Thorpe) – it is highly recommended.** *Tony Wright courtesy of BRM*

Below: **An alternative simple cassette that I have previously used. Screw heads make contact with a piece of printed circuit board (PCB) in a similar position on the main exit from the layout. It worked but not as effectively as the Steve Thorpe idea.** *Author*

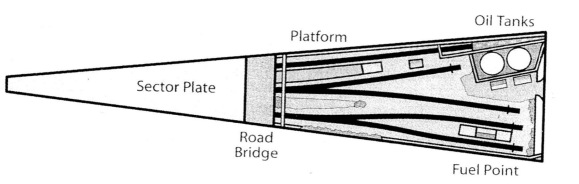

o save space in the hidden area is the 'sector plate', which is pivoted on a bolt and moves in an arc. One very imaginative layout that uses a sector plate is 'Villier Street' by Tony Woods (see the MRM Summer 2005 issue). This EM-gauge layout was constructed as an entry for the DEMU Showcase competition in 2003, and captured the imagination of many people because of its unique perspective on layout design; it won the competition, so must have impressed the judges too! It is a model of a diesel fuelling point and is viewed 'end on'. It is 6 feet long and triangular in shape (see the accompanying plan). The layout is viewed from the base of the triangle and oozes character!

Top: Tony Woods's 'Villier Street', which unusually is triangular in shape and viewed from the right-hand end. *Courtesy of BRM © Dan Wilson, Pacific Studio*

Below: The trackplan of 'Masham', Tony Simms's N-gauge layout. *Courtesy of BRM*

Building a small layout does not mean that you cannot base it on a prototype. One such is 'Masham', an N-gauge layout featured in the November 1999 issue of BRM. For those of us who frequent hostelries, Masham is probably best known today for its two breweries, but the North Eastern Railway built a branch line to it in 1872, which closed in 1963. Tony Simms built a superb 2mm-scale model of Masham, which was constructed in one piece and measured 6 feet by 1ft 6in. The baseboard was made of foamboard (referred to earlier) and Tony obtained his free by using former display boards. The layout is taken to exhibitions and the board has proved to be light, rigid and robust.

My own club, Tywyn MRC, has built two small layouts (one O and one OO gauge) on boards measuring 4 feet by 2ft 8in. The reason for using this size of board is a sad one. One of our members died having built three baseboard frames of those dimensions from 2-by-1-inch timber ready for his new O-gauge layout. We helped his sister dispose

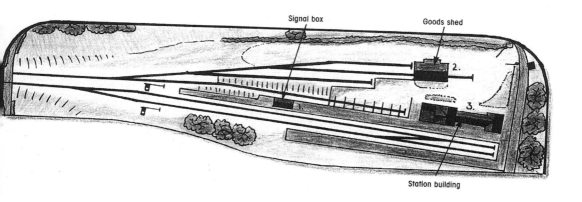

of his railway modelling equipment and stock, and the Club bought the frames.

This leads me to mention what I have often found to be the case for many builders of small layouts. They have a piece of wood, or a baseboard frame, or an odd space at home, and they design a layout to fit it! This, of course, is the opposite of finding a prototype you wish to model, then seeing if you have the space to do it. 'Villier Street' by Tony Woods (mentioned above) and 'Carlton Metals' by Neil Ripley (see Chapter 9) are just two examples of layouts designed to fit a specific area. In both cases they were competition entries where the competition rules specified a certain area measuring so many square feet. The Gauge O Guild has held similar competitions in the past.

Both the Tywyn club layouts are of motive power depots. The OO one ('Neptune Road MPD', named after the road in which our clubroom was located) was based on a design that appeared in *Railway Modeller*. It is operated from the rear. The O-gauge layout was of our own design and is operated from the left-hand end (viewed from the front). They have both given us much pleasure to build and we hope they will give us and the viewing public pleasure when they are at shows. This size of board is about the maximum you can get in a family estate car with all the stock and equipment one has to take to an exhibition.

How you support your layout is obviously a major consideration, especially if you are going to store it and get it out to operate at home or take to exhibitions. One of the most popular methods is to have legs that fold up inside a deep baseboard framework. This means that the layout and its 'support system' are completely self-contained. However, this is not the only method. Trestles ('A frames') can be used, easily made from 2-by-1-inch timber, or a separate supporting framework. A parishioner designed one for me that is shown in three photographs on page 34 of *Layouts for Limited Spaces*. I have used one of those photographs again here, showing the framework fully erected to give an idea of what I am talking about.

Below: **The author's layout support framework (since stained).** *Martin Hewitt*

Alternatively you could use a 'picnic table' – readily bought from places like Focus and B&Q – on which to stand your layout. To get the necessary height for viewing and operating you may need to fit short 'screw-in' legs to the underside of the baseboard. Roger Whitehouse (a fellow Tywyn MRC member) has done this.

Or if you want to be very clever, like Charles Insley, you support your layout on up-turned plastic crates! I say this is very clever because Charles brings his rolling stock and equipment to exhibitions in the crates and simply empties them and turns them upside down to support the layout – simple, cheap and very effective!

Aldi also sells trestles, which are adjustable for height and the legs fold. I have to admit that they are a bit heavy, but they too are very effective!

Having seen them in use at the Stafford Exhibition to support the layout that was behind mine, our club immediately bought four of them at only £9.99 each. If you want them, you need to ask your local Aldi store manager when they are 'coming in', because, like many of the items sold by Aldi, they only appear in the store from time to time.

You can always use an ironing board! As already mentioned, I have done this three times now, and have bought a second-hand one on which to build another! The first time I did this was in 1969, and I have done so again recently. When I built 'Bottrill Street Yard' I also used an ironing board, but made it wider by using 'outriggers' (see the accompanying drawing).

In summary, build what suits *you*! As I have said, I like building layouts depicting engine sheds and depots, but others might like to build models of a goods yard or sidings because they like building wagons. Some people like to build a small terminus, and there are many examples of such layouts at exhibitions and in the model railway press. Narrow-gauge prototypes might take your fancy.

Left: **Roger Whitehouse operating his ingeniously designed layout at a Tywyn MRC exhibition. Note the small screw-in legs – simple but effective.** *David Mitchell*

Below: **My ironing board 'baseboard', with outriggers.** *Peter Honeybone*

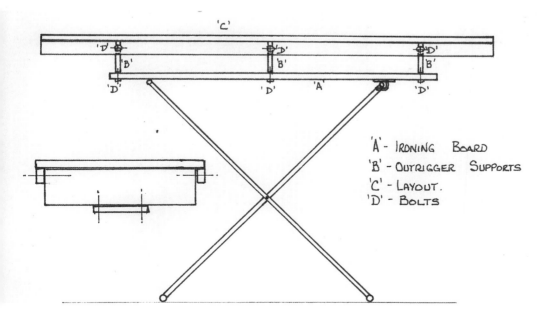

'A' – IRONING BOARD
'B' – OUTRIGGER SUPPORTS
'C' – LAYOUT.
'D' – BOLTS

It really does not matter if you are like me and many other modellers (Ian Futers, for example) who like building a layout, exhibiting it for a few years, then selling it or, if there is no buyer, breaking it up and reusing many of the scenic items such as buildings and figures. I should perhaps also add that sometimes you will build a layout and, when you

have finished it, you don't like it or it isn't as much fun to operate as you thought it was going to be. In

Above and below: **An aerial view/track plan and photograph of 'Bredon', a superb layout that has stood the test of time. This shows that the 6-by-4-foot board still has possibilities, although it is far from easy to transport to shows.** *Both Allan Wood*

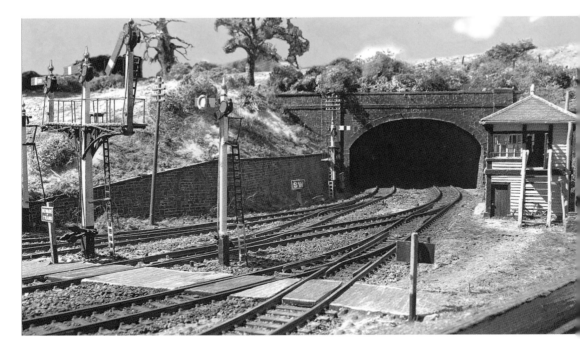

my experience this happens occasionally and is all part of the 'rich tapestry of life'! Just accept it and move on. Very often it is your wife or partner, or a friend who knows you very well, who says something like, 'That's not as good as the other layouts you've built!' In my experience, when this happens they are confirming what you were thinking anyway.

Finally, I should mention that the 6-by-4-foot baseboard, which was so popular for boys building layouts when I was young, can still be used to good effect if you have the space, although it must be said that it is not very portable. A long-standing friend of mine, Allan Wood, built a superb OO-gauge layout ('Bredon') with two friends on such a baseboard. It was described in the September 1981 issue of *Railway Modeller* and was, for a long time, on display at Pecorama. The accompanying photograph shows what a superb layout it is. It is now back with Allan in a garden shed.

To get another view on the building of small layouts, I asked Derek Gelsthorpe to explain his philosophy:

DEREK GELSTHORPE'S PHILOSOPHY

The design and construction of small shunting layouts has been an interest for me for many years. The combination of movements is endless, depending where the points are situated. Three or four points are all that is needed.

My latest layout is 'Idle Way' and is 4 feet by 1 foot in 4mm scale. Only two locos and five trucks are needed to make shunting moves interesting. It can take up to 45 minutes to bring the wagons onto the visible part of the layout, shunt them around and take them back off again. The idea is to place each truck in its particular place, for example goods truck to goods shed and coal truck to coal staithes.

I later introduced an extension with a run-round loop where one loco would be used. I have lost count how many shunting moves I have created – it's like playing chess where you never make the same move twice. It certainly keeps the public interested at exhibitions as there is constant movement.

I originally built small layouts because they took up less space and took less time to complete, but I soon discovered that the same amount of detailing was required. It was not until later that my interest in shunting developed. I have also built a few 'round and round' (continuous) layouts with no sidings. The reason for the lack of sidings is that, in my opinion, you see many layouts with sidings and no movement. If you have sidings they should be used regularly. Continuous layouts attract a lot of people of all ages because they like to see trains moving at scale speed for long distances.

I find that people will stay to look at a small shunting layout if it is operated at very slow speeds and the coupling and uncoupling is not done by a 'big hand from the sky'!

'Sutton Junction' was an N-gauge layout with a 5-foot scenic viewing area and a 1-foot hidden fiddle yard at each end. I could run through trains or shunt wagons. This kept all viewers happy and it was popular at exhibitions.

The other advantage of small layouts is that they are easily transportable and quick to assemble, and do not need much maintenance.

Electrics should be kept as simple as possible. I keep to the same wiring plan and colour code for all my layouts so I can replace a faulty controller within a second, although I have had no problems as yet. I use a method where two wires are secured to each end of the underside of the board with curtain hooks, then wires are passed down through the board from the track to these main wires. If a problem arises it is easy to follow the circuit. This method is called a 'bus bar' system. Two wires are then connected from the bus bar to the DIN plug, where the AC current is also connected, and the controller. All the layouts I have built are totally fictitious but are named after localities within a couple of miles of where I live. It's surprising how many people have crossed that bridge or walked down that road! 'Medental' is a German N-gauge layout with three points and no run-round loop, so two locos are used for shunting.

Uncoupling on all the layouts is by small nails underneath the track, mostly where track joins a set of points. Under the baseboard are permanent magnets, superglued to the nail, which has been cut flush with the board. If I need to uncouple elsewhere I hold a very strong magnet under the

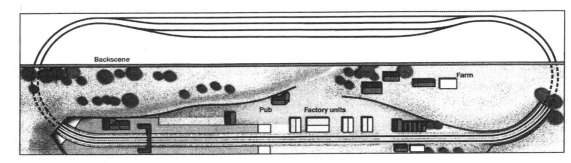

Above and below right: The track plan and a view of Derek Gelsthorpe's Maun Valley 'layout'; the plan shows it as originally built, measuring 9 feet by 2ft 6in. The photographs in this section, provided by Derek Gelsthorpe, illustrate his modelling philosophy and show what a prolific modeller he is of small exhibition layouts in more than one scale and of more than one type. They are all built to the same high standard. (See also 'Idle Way' in Chapter 9.) *Courtesy of BRM/Derek Gelsthorpe*

board. Sprat & Winkle couplings are used as they stay uncoupled to shunt and release the stock.

I think the secret to my slow running is that I don't use a track rubber but a block of wood to clean the rails. The track rubber particles seem to stick to the wheels and track, and also become lodged between rail gaps and points.

A friend said to me many years ago, 'Don't copy someone else's model and use your own ideas', and it has worked for me so far.

'Medental', a German N-gauge layout. *Derek Gelsthorpe*

Two views of Derek Gelsthorpe's 'Rowthorne'. *Both Derek Gelsthorpe*

Above and below: **'Sutton Junction', another Derek Gelsthorpe layout.** *Derek Gelsthorpe*

5
SCENERY AND SCENIC DETAIL

In *Layouts for Limited Spaces* I said that 'small layouts must be strong on scenery and detail so that the attention of the viewing public is held when the movement of rolling stock stops to allow for work in the fiddle yard.' Today I still very much hold to that view.

In these days of digital cameras it is so easy to take photographs of prototype scenery and translate it literally onto your layout if you have the necessary computer skills and equipment. A number of layouts I have seen at exhibitions have back scenes made up from actual photographs. Another use of photographs for backscenes is where calendar photographs have been used to make a montage. When done well it is very effective.

If you do not have these skills there are some very good proprietary backscenes available, such as those from International Models in Llwyngwril, near where I live. I have no connection with Richard and Linda other than as a satisfied customer. The accompanying photograph of a corner of my Gn15 layout, 'Bottrill Street Yard', shows a backscene above the stone wall.

In terms of the layout itself, I have asked Denyse Insley to contribute to this chapter. Her expertise is regularly shared with the exhibition-going members of the public, when she often has a demonstration stand alongside her husband Richard's layout. Her contribution follows, and concerns one of her specialities, wire-frame trees.

Below: **My Gn15 layout 'Bottrill Street Yard' at the Stafford exhibition – note the backscene.** *Author's collection*

Wire-frame trees: variations on a theme

Most modellers will have come across making trees by the wire-frame method. The following is more of the same, but with some individual tweaks and twists.

The method detailed below is suitable for most deciduous trees but not for firs, pines, cypresses, larches, etc, although it can be used to make very realistic Cedars of Lebanon.

What tree?

First you need to decide what sort of tree you are going to make and, having decided, find a picture or photograph that you can refer to. A very good book for this is *The Hamlyn Guide to Trees of Britain and Europe* by C. J. Humphries, J. R. Press and D. A. Sutton (ISBNs 0 7537 0957 0 and 978 0 75370957 3). It shows one half of the tree in leaf and the other half as a 'skeleton'.

You are not going to try and reproduce an exact framework of branches – look at your reference source and decide which are the main branches that give it its distinctive shape; it is the shape that you are aiming for, rather than an exact copy of a living tree.

The process

There are two main procedures involved – well, three if you want to be pedantic: making the frame, preparing the foliage, and finally combining the two. If you don't want to use Sea-foam (aka Forest in a Box) for the foliage, there is a brief description of other foliaging methods at the end.

Sea-foam is a natural plant material and is obtainable from firms such as GreenScene, Gaugemaster and International Models. The preferred one for tree-making by the method being described here is the 'Large' from GreenScene. If you wish to grow and dry your own Sea-foam, the seeds are obtainable from Chiltern Seeds (the botanical name is Telonys aristata).

To prepare the Sea-foam you will need:

- PVA glue; glycerine (obtainable from chemists or cake-decorating shops)
- a large, deep plastic container (preferably with a lid)
- a large, wide-mouthed measuring jug or bucket
- a fine-meshed sieve
- loose scatter material in the colour for the finished tree (medium ground for HO/OO or larger trees, and fine ground for N-gauge trees)
- waxed paper or something similar – it must be smooth, such as the wrappers from some brands of bread
- a 'washing line', on which to hang the drying sprigs, made perhaps from scrap polystyrene, pea-sticks and string
- pegs
- a tray on which the washing line will fit.

Prepare a solution of one part PVA to five parts water, and for every litre of solution you make add 10ml of glycerine. Stir well to ensure that the PVA and glycerine are thoroughly mixed in. Please note that if you strain the solution after use it will keep if not indefinitely then certainly for a good few months, if stored in a cool, dark place in an airtight container.

Soak the Sea-foam sprigs in the solution for at least 2 hours, preferably overnight. For 1 tree about 10 inches high, you will need a minimum of two large Sea-foam sprigs. Make sure that the whole sprig is soaked – if necessary rest a spoon or something similar on top of the sprigs to keep them wholly submerged in the solution.

When the sprigs have had their soaking, take them out individually, shake off the excess solution into the jug or bucket, then, holding the sprig over a piece of waxed paper, sprinkle loose scatter generously over the whole sprig, turning so that all pieces of the sprig are coated. If you wish, carefully remove any leaves on the sprig before you coat it in scatter – it's best to use tweezers to do this.

Next hang the sprig up to dry – allow at least 2 hours for this. If you position the 'washing line' over a piece of waxed paper on a tray, you can recover any scatter that falls off while the sprig is drying.

That's it! Your foliage is prepared and all you
[ne]ed to do now is strain the soaking solution
[thr]ough a sieve to remove any debris and store it
[to] use another time.

[t]he wire frame

[To] make the frame you will need:

- medium- to heavy-weight copper wire,
  depending on the gauge and size of your
  tree. Earthing wire is what you need,
  and this can be obtained quite easily
  from stores such as B&Q.
- * fine copper wire – use welding cable,
  which is heavy-duty electrical equipment
  cable. You may need to go to a specialist
  shop for this – try 'Welding Equipment'
  in Yellow Pages or on the internet. It's
  quite expensive but you don't need long
  lengths, so scrap or off-cuts should be fine
  if you can lay your hands on them.
- florist's stem tape in brown (or green, if
  you can't get brown). Try your local florist
  or florists' wholesaler, or the internet. You
  want the paper sort, Stemtex is the brand
  to look for.
- Humbrol Matt Dark Earth or RailMatch
  Sleeper Grime paint.
- acrylic frame sealant in brown or white,
  depending on what colour you want the
  tree bark to be.
- thick black acrylic craft paint, eg Plaid
  brand.
- artists' tube acrylic colours: red, green, etc.
- powder paint in grey. Liberon does a range
  of Earth colours, but children's powder
  paints are fine – try somewhere like
  Hobbycraft.
- an airtight pot with a lid that comes off
  easily.
- a small spatula such as a tea/coffee stirrer
  or lolly stick.
- a square-cut paintbrush – not your best
  sable, but you need a bit of 'bounce' in the
  bristles so not a stencil brush.
- a jar for water and paper towels.
- a piece of scrap polystyrene, waxed paper
  and pins.

First you need to decide on the size of your
tree. Trees are big, so if you make them to exact
scale they may well look too large when planted on
the layout. If in doubt, make a cardboard cut-out
and try this in position. Generally speaking, scale
down to between two-thirds and three-quarters of
true scale, so a tree that should be 12 inches high
would be scaled down to 8-9 inches.

Next decide how many main branches you need
by looking at your reference source. An HO/OO
tree might need anything from five to nine main
branches, but an N tree might only need three or
four. Cut heavier wires to a little longer than each
of the main branches. Add about 1½ to 2 inches to
the two shortest wires – this forms the planting bit.
Straighten the wires using pliers if they are very
kinked.

Now cut fine wire to the length of the longest
heavier wire plus a bit extra (say 1 to 1½ inches).
Inside welding cable there are bundles: for an HO/
OO tree use 1 to 1½ bundles, and for an N tree use
half a bundle. Untwist the wires but try to keep the
ends level.

You can now start by using one of two
methods.

In the first, you start by twisting the shape of
the tree out of the heavier wires, using two pairs of
pliers to do the very tight twist of the two shortest
main branches at the bottom to which you added
the extra length – this is the planting bit. Then
wrap the fine wires round this frame, sectioning off
little bundles for each main branch.

Alternatively, the heavy and fine wires can
be blended together and the frame and fine wire
branches created as you go along. As soon as

everything is holding together, do the tight twist at the bottom.

This is what your final finished frame should look like.

Branches are formed by wrapping the fine wires round the heavier main branch wires and bringing three or six fine wires out at intervals along the branch, then twisting these to form the subsidiary branches. Do not twist the fine wires all the way along their length – leave them free at the ends.

Note that the fine wires will be far longer than the main branches in the lower part of the tree. What you do therefore is double (or even treble) the wires back on themselves and twist very tightly to make 'lollipops', then cut through the loop so formed so that you have another set of branches. In the photograph above you can see these 'lollipops'

in the middle section of the frame; the lower ones have already been cut through to form extra branches. Make sure that the base of the 'lollipop' is tightly twisted – if it isn't, one branchlet will fall off when you cut through the loop.

At the bottom of the example shown, fine wires have been use to form two small branches without being based on heavier wires.

The next stage is to wrap all the branches, but not the fine wires at the ends of the branches. This hides the twisted wires and gives a base for the next but one stage, which is the coating.

For the wrapping you need florist's tape. This is cut into strips about 3 inches long, then usually cut in half along the length. This makes it easier to manipulate, but if you are making a very large tree

you could use longer lengths straight off the roll. Florist's tape is slightly tacky, so you don't need to use glue.

Look at your wire frame and decide which of the main branches is going to be to be the final one to be wrapped; this is because this final wrap will catch in all the ends from the other branches on the trunk. In the photograph above the branch at the top left will be the last one to be wrapped.

Apply this principle to all of the main branches so that the final wrapping on each branch ends on the trunk. Start wrapping at the topmost branch nearest the final one to be wrapped and make sure that you end the wrap on the main branch. Work downwards and inwards. Stretch the florist's tape gently as you work and, at the start, roll the end between your fingers so that you have something to grab the branch with. Make sure that you cover the previous end when starting a new piece of tape, and make sure that you end on the trunk.

Don't be afraid to push branches out of the way until you come to them. Having made the basic form, you can always restore them when needed.

Finally, wrap all the way down the trunk from the bare branch left at the top, making sure that you catch in all the ends from the other main branches.

The photograph above shows a completely wrapped tree. Now paint the fine bare wires at the ends of the branches with Humbrol Matt Dark Earth or Railmatch Sleeper Grime; you may find it quicker to do this using eye-shadow applicators, available from chemists, rather than a paintbrush. It's useful here to go over the tree before you start and make sure that all the fine wires are separated, as they do tend to get tangled up during the wrapping process. Start painting at the top and work downwards. Again, don't be afraid to pull the branches out of position; florist's tape is flexible and you can put them back into place later.

The next stage is to coat the wrapped frame with acrylic frame sealant and the photograph shows the equipment needed.

First you need to prepare the frame sealant. Use brown if you are making a tree with a dark trunk, or white/grey if it has a light trunk. The base must be acrylic – silicone-based sealants won't work.

Place a good squeeze of the frame sealant into a small airtight pot with a lid that is easily removed, then use small amounts of acrylic craft paint and artist's acrylic tube paints to get the colour you want. If the mixture seems to be getting a bit too runny, add some powder paint. Mix the colours into the frame sealant base very well – it may take a little while and 'elbow grease' to get them mixed in completely. Test the colour by putting a smear on a bit of paper and let it dry, but remember that frame sealant dries very quickly once out of the tube, so keep the pot of mixed sealant covered at all times when not in use. If the colour is not quite right, adjust it by adding more pigment, but try to avoid adding excessive amounts as this will alter the flexible quality of the sealant.

When you are satisfied with the colour, start painting the sealant on the frame, starting at the top and working downwards and inwards. Using the spatula/cocktail stick, put a small dab of the sealant onto the branch you are going to coat and push it roughly into position, meanwhile keeping the sealant pot covered. Dip your paint brush in water and dry it off on kitchen paper so that it is not dripping, then smooth the sealant on and around the branch. Do not try to coat the fine wires at the ends of the branches. When you have finished that section, put the paintbrush back into the jar of water and give it a good shake to remove any excess sealant adhering to it. In fact, you will probably have to give the brush a thorough cleaning a few

times in the course of coating the whole tree.

In this photograph the top right-hand branch has been coated. Stick the frame in a piece of scrap polystyrene once coating has started. Note that while you can push the lower branches out of the way as a temporary measure whilst coating the upper part of the tree, they should be brought back into position before they get their own coating. Also remember that when you are not using the sealant, keep it covered, and if you are not using your paintbrush, keep it in water.

When you have coated the lowest branches but before you coat the lower trunk, take a piece of polystyrene, which should be big enough to hold the tree frame without toppling over (and make sure that it is deep enough to take the tightly twisted planting bit at the bottom), and prepare it by covering the top with a piece of waxed paper (waxed side up) and anchor the paper with pins. Then take your partly coated tree frame and stick it firmly into the block through the waxed paper; the planting end should be completely buried in the polystyrene and the trunk should meet the paper (see the photographs below). Use your spatula/cocktail stick like a palette knife to finish off the trunk, bringing the sealant out onto the waxed paper. If you give it a little time so that the sealant begins to dry, you can get really good texture into the trunk at this stage by using a nearly dry paintbrush or cocktail stick. Once the lower trunk has been coated, put the frame on one side to dry thoroughly; the branches will dry quite

quickly because you don't need a particularly thick coat (unless you are bulking up the branch), but the lower trunk will take longer because the sealant will be thickest there.

When the frame has completely dried you can, if you wish, dry-brush it or use Carr's powders to highlight the texture or to indicate a north-facing side by adding a hint of green.

That's it – your frame is complete and you will find that the branches and, to some extent, the trunk will remain completely flexible.

Adding foliage

For a tree as shown in the photograph you will need:

- prepared Sea-foam foliage
- UHU Power Glue or similar
- angled tweezers
- scissors

The photograph shows the start of foliaging a tree with prepared Sea-foam foliage. Basically what you do is break off sections from the prepared sprig, trim

them up and glue them to the prepared frame.

Start at the top and work downwards. Once more, you can gently push the lower branches out of the way and bring them back into position when it's their turn to be foliaged.

The glue should be applied to the fine wires and part way down the branch (check by putting the piece of Sea-foam in place first without the glue), then attach the Sea-foam piece by sliding it into place, making sure that the fine wires penetrate it so that it is held firmly. You may need to hold the piece onto the branch until the glue sets (that's why the tweezers are invaluable – you don't want to glue your fingers as well as the foliage!), so a quick-setting glue is essential.

The photograph shows a completed tree. When you have finished the foliage, look at the tree and, if there are any obvious gaps, fill them with more foliage, or if there are any obvious places where you can see glue (it happens – oh yes, it does!), cover it with a dab of prepared frame sealant

Finally, apply a coating of cheap hairspray if you wish and gently ease the tree off the waxed paper with your thumbnail so that you have a little flexible base for when you plant it in the layout.

Other types of foliage

Reindeer moss (lichen) is a good old stand-by, coated with loose scatter. Use brown lichen to match the frame as far as possible. Select nice bushy pieces, not straggly, leggy ones, and attach them to the frame using UHU Power Glue or similar by coating the fine wires and branches and firmly pushing the lichen in place. When the frame has been covered with lichen, wrap the trunk as much as you can with clingfilm and spray all over with a spray glue (3M Display Mount is a good one to use) and immediately cover generously with loose scatter. Allow to dry thoroughly. If necessary, reapply the spray glue and scatter to any bare patches, and finally give a good coating of cheap hairspray. Remove the clingfilm and ease the frame off the waxed paper.

Another option is foliage net, a loose scatter on a base, produced by Woodland Scenics (look for packets with a square inch measurement of the contents), GreenScene, Heki, etc. This is really best for trees with markedly horizontal branches such as Cedars of Lebanon, but can be use for other trees, particularly in N scale.

Basically, all you do is glue pieces onto the finished wire frame, building them up in layers if necessary to add bulk. Again, a final coating of cheap hairspray is helpful as foliage nets do tend to shed their scatter.

Other scenic details

Pictures are often much better than words at showing what we mean, so there follows a selection of photographs of scenic detail on layouts and some prototype detail, which I hope, together with the captions, will explain why I so strongly believe that scenery and scenic detail are very important.

One final point: Bachmann and Hornby now produce some fantastic OO and N gauge ready-made buildings and figures that can be 'personalised' by painting doors and windows different colours or by being 'dirtied up', depending on what you are trying to portray. Such buildings are not available in O gauge, but you can still get kits from manufacturers like Metcalfe and Heljan; the former are card and the latter plastic.

Left: This photograph was taken in Africa, and look at the detail! Logs, flowers, a wooden shed and a water tower, and none of it looks out of place. *David Mitchell*

Below: Another picture from Africa, this time showing locos being prepared. Note the man standing on the oil drum, which would undoubtedly be frowned upon today in the UK! *David Mitchell*

Bottom: At Llangollen in April 2009 the detail is for all to see: the pit, the upside-down wheelbarrow, the buried sleepers, the oil tank, the oil drums and the wooden pallets. *Author*

Above: Photographed at Loughborough in May 2009 are two stacks of pallets and rubbish under the bridge, together with all the fire irons hanging on the pier. So atmospheric! *Author*

Above and left: Another Loughborough scene, showing a storage compound for gas bottles and the mesh fence behind – a common site but not often modelled. *Author*

Top: Also photographed at Loughborough in May 2009 are a grounded van body, a modern building behind the mesh fence, corrugated sheet, oil drums and a bench (with a leg that isn't straight!) with a vice on it. *Author*

Above: 'Clutter' at its best – a picture that says it all! *Author*

Right: More general clutter beneath the trees at Llangollen, including a different kind of fence, oil drums, trolleys on their side and bits of wood. *Author*

p: Preparing for tracklaying the approach to Rhydyronen. te the different colours the ballast, the new rail gths on the left-hand side d the new Jarrah sleepers on e right, all ready for the gang start work.

R collection

ddle: This is Wharf station the TR. Note the loco on e coal road, the vehicles, the rkers, the tipper wagons, e water tank, the removed ndard-gauge track along the arf, the oil drum, the grass, d weeds growing between e standard-gauge rails.

R collection

low: Pendre in the snow: have included this picture r those who want to model snow scene, which is very fective when done well, as me exhibition layouts show. ote how the snow has not mpletely covered the clutter the West Shed and the rails the loco (No 7 *Tom Rolt*).

ul Shuttleworth, TR collection

Right: In my opinion, this picture taken on the back road at the TR's Pendre Works 'oozes atmosphere'! *David Mitchell*

Below: Pendre again – this time loco No 6 in unusual livery and facing Wharf for a change is getting the empty coaching stock out of the North Shed. Note the sleeper-drilling rig by the Guard, the big pile of fencing posts by the shed, the rusty rail lengths and the corrugated fence. *TR collection*

Bottom: I have included this picture to show the slate fencing that is very common on Welsh narrow-gauge railways in the areas where slate was mined. *TR collection*

A wonderful trio of pictures of 'clutter' at Pendre! It is adding this sort of detail to a layout that I find very rewarding. *All TR collection*

Above: Now here are some examples of the kind of detail jus[t] seen being translated into model form. This an overall view of my layout 'The Shed' at the Sutton Coldfield exhibition in 2009. *Author*

Left: A view of the yard on 'The Shed'. The terraced house[s] are a Metcalfe kit (sadly these kits are no longer made i[n] O gauge). Note the men at the back door, sawing woo[d] and leaning on a broom, the two ladies having a chat, th[e] container and the Austin Allegro. *Author*

Right: The background water tank hides the exit to the cassette area of 'The Shed'. Note the bench inside the shed, the man filling his bucket from the tank outside the shed, and many other people going about their work. *Author*

Left: Another view of 'The Shed', this time looking the other way. Note the man working on the roof and the associated ladders, the man breaking up the rubbish in the skip, the 'Portakabin', the cars – and the Fat Controller! *Author*

Right: A view of 'Wyken Yard', a layout built in the 1990s. Note the two men changing a tyre on the milk float, the pallets, the man breaking up rubbish in the skip (again!) and also the drain holes in the retaining wall, made from drinking straws. The excuse for the bus and Morris Minor Traveller is a company restoring old vehicles! *Martin Hewitt*

Below: A photo of one of my earlier layouts, again showing the clutter and scenic detail. It even includes a man relieving himself by the oil drums! *Martin Hewitt*

Above: **A view of my layout 'Frankwell Street Yard'. Note the container on sleepers, the man standing in the hole by the loco talking to his supervisor, and the gang in high-visibility overalls having a break.** *Tony Wright, courtesy of British Railway Modelling*

Left: **A view of Mike Bragg's layout 'Lenche Bridge' – note the hole in the roof and the super half-sunk barge.** *Author*

Right: **A view of 'Seahouses' by Kevin Cartwright – not a loco in sight, but look at the atmosphere! It is helped by the fact that the building is lit.** *Tony Wright, courtesy of British Railway Modelling*

6
ROLLING STOCK FOR SMALL LAYOUTS

It is perhaps stating the obvious that it is highly unlikely that you will run large locos and rolling stock on a small layout. As illustrated in Chapter 4, it is possible to have a large loco and coach running through your station, but that presumes that the hidden sidings, cassette, sector plate or whatever you use is long enough to accommodate them.

Normally, if you are going to build a small layout, either through choice or because of a lack of space, you will design it with the rolling stock you are going to be using very much in mind.

The type of layout you have is also affected by the rolling stock you use. For example, I have said

that I like building models of small loco sheds or stabling points. Therefore I take into account the fact that there are a fair number of O-gauge locos on the market that are less than 8 inches long. So, the length of dead sections on such a layout would be a maximum length of 8 inches. It sounds a bit basic, and of course it is, but sometimes we forget the basics. If you have the odd loco that is longer, provided that the wheelbase is no more than 8 inches it can still be used; it just means that it will overhang the section on either side of it. This is where the planning of your operating sequence comes in – simply allow for the fact that one or more of your locos will overhang the next section. It is also possible to allow for a loco up to 16 inches long when planning the sequence by allocating two

Below: **One of Neil Burgess's locos on his 'Blagdon' layout. Just to confuse matters, the loco is also named *Blagdon*!** *Steve Flint, courtesy of Railway Modeller*

dead sections to it when it is stationary. I should add, of course, that the cassette or sector plate has to be able to accommodate the large loco too.

As mentioned earlier, if your interest is building wagons you could build a layout representing a wagon works. Simply discover the length of the average wagon or van and design the layout accordingly. You could model a set of sidings (see 'Tryweryn' in Chapter 9).

Right: A kit-built diesel from Back 2 Bay 6 on my Gn15 layout. The chassis (Tenshodo 'Spud') is fixed with Blu-Tack! *Author*

Below: Two more locos on my Gn15 layout. The one with the cab is another Back 2 Bay 6 kit and the open-cab one is a converted Triang loco. The poster advertising Harlech Castle is from an Arriva Trains (Wales) Ltd postcard featuring three different posters – all you have to do is cut them out! *Author*

I also have built a small Gn15 layout (see 'Bottrill Street Yard' in Chapter 9), where the little locos will easily go round a 6-inch radius curve, and the wagons have a short wheelbase too, so there is another option for the space-starved modeller.

If you are starting to build your layout from scratch or have decided to change scales, I think it pays to buy a few locos and wagons and design your layout with the rolling stock very much in mind. In N, OO and increasingly in O gauge there is a good 'ready-to-run' rolling stock market, so it is easy to obtain a few 'samples'. For example, I model mainly in O gauge, and Skytrex produce some excellent small locos and wagons; I have 'Toby the Tram', a Sentinel and, in modern image, an O2 diesel.

Left: **A Skytrex Sentinel on my 'Frankwell Street Yard' layout.** *Tony Wright, courtesy of British Railway Modelling*

Above: **Four small locos on one of my former engine shed layouts: a tram loco, a diesel, an 0-6-0 steam loco and an Atlas diesel repainted. All these are short-wheelbase locos because the dead sections on the layout were only 7 inches long.** *Martin Hewitt*

Left: **Two diesels on the layout in my spare room.** *Author*

Three small locos on my O-gauge layout 'Bottrill Street Yard'. Note also the scenic detail in these three photographs.
All Tony Wright, courtesy of British Railway Modelling

7

EXHIBITING YOUR LAYOUT

As I said at the beginning of this book, a small layout is much easier to exhibit than a large one because it can be easily transported in a family [saloon]. visitors see layouts that could be accommodated in their homes. In my earlier book, *Layouts for Limited Spaces*, I briefly described what is involved if you are invited to exhibit your layout. Basically it can be summed up as follows.

You receive an invitation, you decide to accept and you put the date(s) in your diary! Ensure that the exhibition manager has your 'exhibition handout' (layout details sheet); if you haven't got one, prepare one (see the example reproduced here).

Ensure that you have all the information you need about the exhibition and that your estimate of expenses is submitted. To help in this most exhibition managers have a 'pro-forma' for you to complete, which gives them all the information they require (again, see the accompanying example).

Left: **The 'exhibition handout' for my layout 'The Shed'.**

Below: **A 'pro-forma' sent to prospective exhibitors at the Tywyn & District MRC exhibition.**

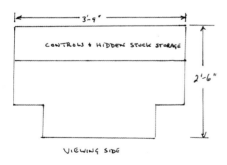

THE SHED

Owner: Revd Nigel Adams

Address:

Scale / gauge: 0

Size: 3' 9'' x 2' 6'' plus operating space. (includes small front extension 8'' deep)
Now supported on a framework instead of Ironing Board 'legs' as per photo.

Requirements: 1 x 13amp power point
1 small table for stock if possible

Number of operators: 2

Insurance: £1250

Description for exhibition guides.
In the mid 1960s I built an 009 layout on an ironing board and it seemed to generate quite a bit of interest at exhibitions. In the Summer of 2007 I was passing our local 'end of line shop' and noticed an ironing board for sale for £6. I bought it with the intention of trying to fit an 0 gauge layout onto it!
What you see before you is the result. It is probably an overstatement to call it a layout – perhaps a better description is a 'working diorama'. Whatever you call it, it is simply 2 lengths of track with a cassette area at each end and depicts part of a loco shed. It was simple and quick to build and, as usual for me, I spent a long time adding scenic detail including lights in two of the low relief buildings, and an arcwelder and a flashing light in two other buildings. There is a 'Can you find list' for those who like that sort of thing. Since I built the layout I have added a small 8'' deep scenic extension at the front to give it a bit more depth.
The Shed is operated to a sequence timetable and I personally find it quite relaxing to shuffle the locos around. If you have any questions please ask the operator. One of the reasons I called it 'The Shed' is that I had a previous layout of that name and still had the professionally made nameboard for it and it seemed a shame to waste it!

It is also cheaper for exhibition managers because it does not need so many operators to [ru]n it and it does not need a van to be hired to [tr]ansport it.

I personally think that having a number of [sm]all layouts at an exhibition also ensures that the

Make sure that your layout is working properly and clean all the stock just before the show. When you load the car I believe a check list is vital to make sure that you leave nothing behind. Even if you make all the necessary preparations, you might still forget something – all you have done is minimised the risk! If you do forget something, you will find fellow exhibitors are always ready to help if they can; after all, they might want you to return the favour one day. (Even with a check list my friend and I once drove off to a show having left the lighting rig against the garden wall while we loaded something else!). Also, take spares – for example, controller, AC transformer, light bulbs – and a notebook to note down any work you need to do on the layout or stock when you return

Above: My Gn15 layout, stock box, tool box, trestles and all that I take to a show stacked up in the dining room, ready to be loaded into the car. *Author*

Below: My check list for 'The Shed', used for three exhibition outings.

Above: Stock boxes come in different designs, shapes and sizes but are vital to avoid damage to stock travelling to and from shows. This is one of Justin's stock boxes (made from an old record case!); it contains three wooden trays that stack one on top of each other. *Author*

THE SHED (IRONING BOARD) EXHIBITION CHECKLIST

Layout with protection pieces fitted	✓	✓	·
Record Player box	x	x	✓
Picnic Box	✓	✓	x
3 Tier trolley on wheels	✓	✓	·
Grey folding box on wheels	✓	✓	
The Shed cardboard box	✓	✓	✓
LAYOUT EXTENSION	✓		
Exhibition instructions and paperwork	✓	✓	x
FOLDING TROLLEY (FOR LAYOUT)	X	x	·
Overnight bag/case (if required)	x	✓	x
Shoulder bag or rucksack	✓	o/s	x
Cheque book	✓	✓	x
TOM WALL BANK SUPPORT FRAME	✓	✓	
Battery Operated Vacuum Cleaner	✓	·	✓
2 black frontals (in 3 tier trolley)	✓	✓	✓
Folding Table	x	·	·
Wheel cleaning cradle, brush and Gloves	✓	✓	✓
Tool Box	✓	✓	✓
Folding stool	✓	✓	
Grey plastic crates (lights etc) No 3	✓	✓	·
Small roll of carpet	✓	✓	X
Small blue briefcase	✓	✓	✓
BOX OF VEHICLES FOR LKTN	✓	·	·
SILVER LOCO STOCK BOX		✓	✓

right: **One of my stock boxes, using the same principle as ustin's example; this time the wooden trays fit inside a large oolbox.** *Author*

ght: **This large stock box was andmade (not by me!).** *Author*

ght: **A stock box for the farquhar Branch' layout built Revd W. Awdry many years o. The layout is now in the R Museum at Wharf and is ailable for shows. Note the e of corrugated cardboard as viders.** *Steve Thorpe*

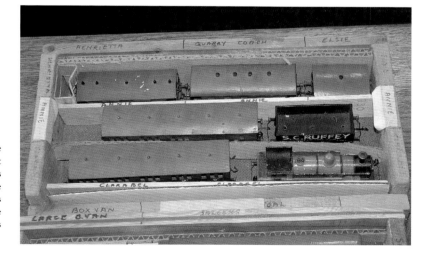

home. If an overnight stop is required, don't forget your case!

Take the map showing where the exhibition venue is located; exhibition managers usually send you this when confirming your attendance about four weeks before the exhibition.

Despite all the hard work, preparation, travelling, setting up and dismantling the layout, not forgetting the 6 or 7 hours per day operating the layout, I still thoroughly enjoy exhibiting. You meet fellow enthusiasts and exhibitors and you talk to many interesting people. You may even get some complimentary remarks about your layout!

Whatever your personal preferences, I believe that the vast number of people visiting exhibitions expect to see something running on a layout. On small layouts this is not as easy as, say, on a large multi-track 'round-and-round' layout, but as long as something is moving most of the time, people appear to be satisfied.

This is also where scenic detail helps – people can look at that while you are moving stock around in the hidden sidings. I always have a 'Can you find…?' list on the front of the layout; I find that adults and children alike will readily try and spot the listed items. One word of warning – ensure

that there is an 'answer sheet' on the layout for your fellow operators, if they were not involved in adding the scenic detail! This is particularly true in my case. My elder son Justin regularly operates my layout at shows, but he and I live 140 miles apart and so he needs the 'answer sheet'.

I am one of those people who much prefer to have a sequence of moves to follow, which, in my case, are set out on flip-over cards fixed to a ring binder from an old A4 file. In this way I know that at the end of the sequence, all the stock should be back where it needs to be to restart the sequence again (unless I have made a mistake!). Also, it means that I can have a conversation with a visitor without having to remember where I was in the sequence before we started the conversation. The sequence need not be long – most of mine have between 20 and 35 moves.

One thing I have not mentioned is tidiness at exhibitions. Because you will have taken a layout support system (maybe trestles), stock boxes, a tool box, spares and so on, the area round the layout can begin to look very untidy. To ensure this does not happen, most exhibitors take a frontal screen that wraps round the layout from one end to the other, fixed with drawing pins or Velcro. Not only does this make the layout look tidy, it improves the presentation and you can store all your equipment under the layout where it is hidden from view.

I also usually take a small folding table with me so that I can put a stock box on it behind the layout. This avoids having to dive under the layout for another loco if one starts 'playing up' or fails.

Lighting is also essential as some exhibition venues are poorly lit. Some people have light hidden behind fascias, but I have found the small clip-on halogen lights are so much easier to use and I have never had any complaints from visitors about the 'light getting in their eyes', as you certainly would with the old kind of spotlights. The clip-on lights that I use are also adjustable, being flexible.

Left: A typical 'Can you find…?' list to entertain visitors between loco movements.

Opposite: My 'Frankwell Street Yard' layout at the Chapel-en-le-Frith show. Note the operating sequence cards in the top left of the photo. *Author*

Inset: The arrangement of flip-over cards using a ring-binder from an old A4 file. *Peter Honeybone*

CAN YOU FIND THE FOLLOWING:-

- **Man at the foot of a ladder**

- **Man and a ladder on the roof**

- **Man carrying a ladder**

- **2 red gas cylinders**

- **Gas cylinder on a trolley**

- **Man at workbench (2)**

- **5 white loco lamps and 2 black ones**

- **2 red buckets**

- **A bicycle**

- **9 Oil drums**

- **Man crouching by a grey bucket**

- **Man standing with his coat over his left shoulder**

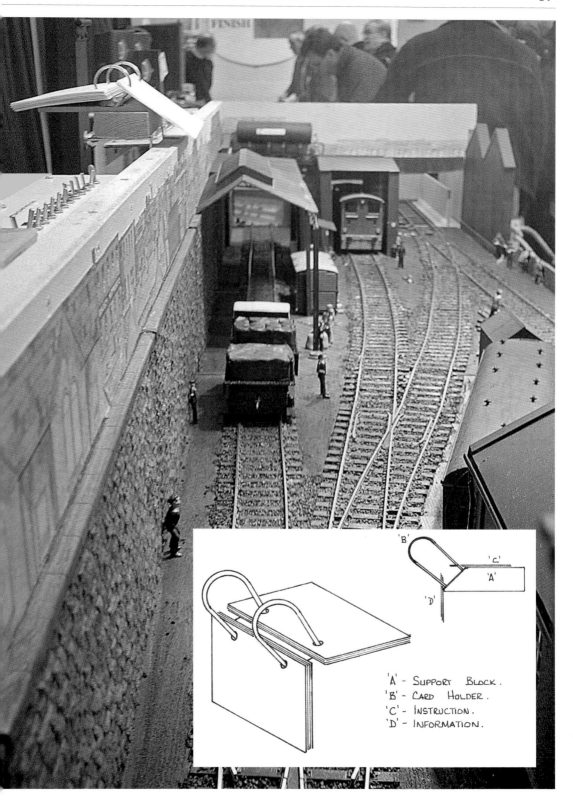

'A' - SUPPORT BLOCK.
'B' - CARD HOLDER.
'C' - INSTRUCTION.
'D' - INFORMATION.

Above: **Me and my elder son Justin operating 'The Shed' at Tywyn MRC's 2009 exhibition.** *Paul Gunn*

Setting up a layout and dismantling it is a 'necessary evil' and is obviously unavoidable. If you do it in a logical sequence it becomes less of a chore and there is something quite satisfying when you have set it up and it works first time!

One final point: you will have your bad days when things go wrong. They are unavoidable. All you can do is minimise the risk by proper preparation. However, the good days far outweigh the bad. I exhibited one of my layouts at a show and all was working perfectly. Suddenly, out of the blue, one of the points apparently failed. The problem was clearly electrical but nothing was obviously wrong. Worse still, the fault was intermittent, and intermittent faults are always the most difficult to locate. My fellow operator had much more electrical 'know-how' than me

and even he was totally non-plussed. Eventually after about 2 hours of this intermittent fault, we traced it to a dry solder joint!

Left and above: These three photos were also taken at Tywyn MRC's 2009 exhibition. Exhibiting a layout is very enjoyable, but occasionally gremlins have their say! They are Tywyn MRC's 'Neptune Road MPD' (left), Newtown MRS's 'Hudson's Wharf' (top), and Martin Rich's 'Nearleigh Works' (above). *All Paul Gunn*

8
WHY NOT JOIN A CLUB?

The simple answer may be that there isn't one in your area, which can be true in sparsely populated areas of the country. The other answer might be that you don't feel that you are 'the model railway club type'. If that is the case, fine.

However, by belonging to a club you will meet fellow railway modellers and you will be able to 'pick their brains' on areas of modelling that are not your strong points. For example, Bob, a fellow member of Tywyn MRC, is my guru when it comes to the 'electrics'. I can manage the basics well enough, but I turn to Bob if I have a problem. My particular interests are scenic detail and compiling operation sequences, so, in return, I have helped Bob with those aspects when he has built layouts.

Of course, if the club itself is building a layout or layouts, all the members put in their share of their particular interest or expertise. They also provide a ready-made pool of operators if you exhibit you layout; it is not possible to exhibit a layout – even if it only requires one operator – without having a relief for meals and toilet breaks if nothing else In my experience, fellow members like taking a layout to an exhibition, even if they have not done it before. They soon get used to what is involved For example, the minimum number of operator for my small layouts is two for a one-day show and three for a longer show. This is not unreasonable and gives the operators time not only for meal and toilet breaks, but also, of course, to look round the exhibition.

If there is no club in your area, why no consider starting one? In the last 43 years I have done that three times, and each of the clubs is stil

Above: **Tywyn MRC members (and a visitor from Hull MRS, Neil Ripley, extreme right) behind the Club's 'Common Lane Wharf' layout in 2007. Belonging to a club is a great way of** sharing your hobby, learning from others and meeting fellow enthusiasts. *Paul Gunn*

in existence. My present club (Tywyn & District MRC) has a small membership because we live in a sparsely populated area, but the other two clubs I founded have much larger memberships because they are located in the Midlands. Some members travel more than 20 miles to Tywyn, and this also applies to the O-gauge group of which my elder son is a member.

I personally think it is well worth the effort to join a club – or even found one. Another bonus is that the club programmes often include interesting talks, slide shows, and so on.

Finally, if you have absolutely no space at all at home for your layout, which is very rare, you can carry out your modelling activities at a club.

Right: **Lord Dafydd Elis-Thomas (the Presiding Officer of the Welsh Assembly) performing the official opening of the new clubroom of Tywyn & District Model Railway Club on 30 January 2010.** *Paul Gunn*

Below: **Members of Tywyn & District Model Railway Club with Lord Dafydd Elis-Thomas and Mr Peter Saunders (Peter Saunders Trust) after the opening.** *Paul Gunn*

9
SMALL LAYOUTS GALLERY

Dolgoch

This is a layout with a difference in five respects. It was built to be the centrepiece of the stand that the London Area Group of the Talyllyn Railway Preservation Society had at the Model Railway Clubs Annual Exhibition at Central Hall, Westminster, in April 1956. It is therefore now well over 50 years old and still going strong!

It was built to 4mm scale and the track gauge is 8mm; the track was obviously hand built because this was long before the advent of commercially available 009 track. It operated automatically (and still does) or manually if required. It was (and is) totally enclosed in an illuminated cabinet, which earned it two nicknames: the 'Aquarium' and the 'Fish Tank'!

As there were then no readily available small

electric motors to fit into the model of loco No 3 (*Si Haydn*), a Triang X04 motor was adapted to fit int Van No 5 (the brake-van/booking office), and this i permanently coupled to No 3.

The layout was built by the late Keith Banniste and, although it was somewhat foreshortenec compared to the prototype in order to allow it to be transported to and from shows, it really captures the atmosphere of the prototype, which was very differen back in the 1950s when compared to today.

Over more than half a century the only majo changes to the layout have been the addition of the

Below and above right: **The first of these two photographs** the Dolgoch 'diorama' shows the small train in the station remember that the motor is not in the loco but in the brake van (No 5). The second picture shows the train crossing the viaduct, which, of course, is *the* feature of Dolgoch. Bo *Justin Adams*

footbridge leading to Dolgoch Falls (and that was 51 years ago!) and a partial scenic renovation in 1982. It was 'mothballed' from some time in the mid-1960s until 1982 when it 'came out of retirement' to be shown at an exhibition in Shrewsbury. The automatic operation lacks the smoothness that one might expect from modern-day electronics, but that is hardly surprising – it was way ahead of its time when built in 1956. The train does one circuit of the track, stops in the station for 2 minutes, then does another circuit, and so it carries on all day! For those that understand such things – which I don't – it is controlled by dropping resistors across the rails which, in turn, are controlled by a 'Uniselector', which I understand was used in telephone exchanges in the 1950s. The timer is from an aircraft.

The builders must have had great faith in the scratch-built stock because there are no spares at all! The train consists of No 3 *Sir Haydn* hauling the three original Brown Marshall coaches and the brake-van delivered to the Talyllyn Railway in 1865. Normally the loco works chimney-first towards Towyn (1950s spelling) as it did in the early 1950s on the real thing, compared with today when locos work chimney-first up the line to Nant Gwernol – which

wasn't even open in the 1950s (the extension from Abergynolwyn opened in 1976).

The layout was built to be transported in two halves and it stands on short legs – usually on a 6-by-2-foot table provided by the exhibition venue. It is 72 inches long by 21 inches wide, and 18½ inches high. The panels that make up the 'cabinet' slide into runners.

There is even a 'clock' that tells you how many circuits have been completed by the train in a day. From available records, the train has done between 248 and 430 circuits per day at exhibitions. When Keith Bannister died in 2001 the layout was stored in a TR volunteer's home, and when he died it was given back to the TRPS.

Myself and a fellow member, Bob Hey, changed the mains input and a little of the wiring for a modern power input, but we left the original mains wiring and transformer in situ so as to preserve the layout as it was built.

If any exhibition managers read this book and would like the layout to appear at an exhibition, they should contact me or Steve Thorpe c/o the Talyllyn Railway, Wharf Station, Tywyn, Gwynedd LL36 9EY.

For obvious reasons we have to limit the number of shows it attends, but we will always try and oblige.

We also have Rev Wilbert Awdry's famous 'Ffarquhar Branch', which can also be exhibited. This too has been refurbished. Writing as a working volunteer of 26 years, I hope it goes without saying that if either layout is exhibited we would wish to bring TR timetables and publicity material too.

Two photographs of Rev Awdry 'Ffarquhar Branch' layout, which has been refurbished and can b exhibited. *Both TR collection*

Idle Way

Derek Gelsthorpe has built a number of excellent layouts in N gauge, but this one, in OO gauge, certainly qualifies for the description 'layout in a limited space'.

It is called 'Idle Way' and is a minimum-space layout for use at home and at exhibitions. It is a model of a shunting yard and uses readily available track, building kits and scenic accessories, so is very suitable as an example for a beginner.

You need to be the sort of person who likes shunting wagons round a yard to enjoy this sort of layout and, if you are like me, you would follow a sequence of moves written out on cards. The layout measures just 4 by 1 feet with a small add-on section at the left-hand end and a removable single 'fiddle track' at the right-hand end.

The main board was originally built as a self-contained unit, ,but Derek added the left-hand extension to allow him to extend the two sidings at that end to allow longer trains to access the two kick-back sidings. He has also added a scenic extension to the front, which depicts a canal scene.

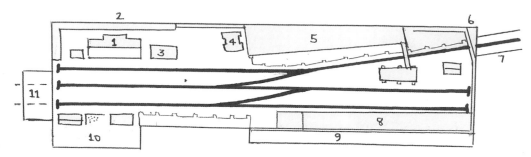

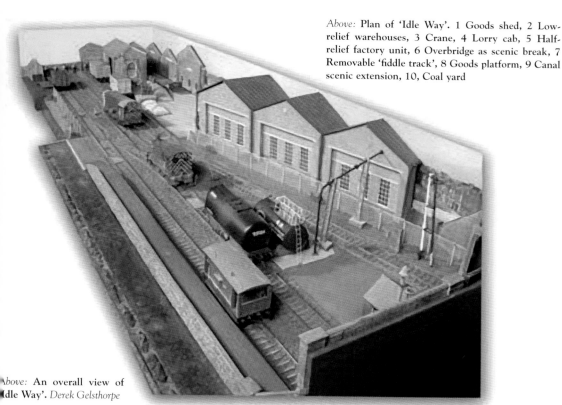

Above: **Plan of 'Idle Way'.** 1 Goods shed, 2 Low-relief warehouses, 3 Crane, 4 Lorry cab, 5 Half-relief factory unit, 6 Overbridge as scenic break, 7 Removable 'fiddle track', 8 Goods platform, 9 Canal scenic extension, 10, Coal yard

Above: **An overall view of Idle Way'.** *Derek Gelsthorpe*

Above: **A close up of two diesel locos on 'Idle Way'.** *Derek Gelsthorpe*

The track plan is very simple and uses four Peco medium-radius points. They are operated by dowelling rods that run through the sideframes of the baseboard and protrude at both the front and the back; the layout can therefore be operated from either side. The point tie bar is connected to the dowel rod by stiff steel wire, one end of which fits into a hole drilled into the rod and the other fits into the hole in the tie bar. Electrics are very simple, and there are only four feeds and two dead sections.

The track is glued to the baseboard and ballasted with Woodland Scenics' grey and brown ballast with the usual mixture of PVA glue thinned down with water. Unlike many modellers, Derek doesn't add a drop or two of detergent to break down the surface tension. To ensure a straight edge to the ballast, masking tape is laid alongside the outside of the track. The glue is applied by syringe between the tape and the edge of the ballast, and is drawn into the ballast by capillary action. When it is dry the tape can be removed, leaving a neat edge. Derek also applied various colours of thinned paint to give the whole area a weathered appearance

In the yard he used a mixture of black and white Humbrol paint, and before the paint dried it was brushed over with talcum powder to represent tarmac.

Derek uses stock fitted with Sprat & Winkle couplings, which are operated by permanent magnets glued under the track in the required positions. The couplings have a delayed action which means that, once the coupling on the wagon is pulled down by the magnet, it can be shunted anywhere along the length of the siding and will not recouple.

Derek deliberately made the shunting moves complicated because that is what he likes, and he only uses two locos, five wagons and a brake-van in the operating sequence.

I think there are a number of advantages to building a small layout such as 'Idle Way'. It is small and easily transportable; it can be finished and operated in a reasonably short time; it uses readily available track, buildings and scenic materials; it is simple to wire up; and it does not require specialist skills. Nevertheless it is a very effective little layout and, as it is regularly exhibited, shows newcomers to the hobby and those with very little space in the home that such layouts are fun to build and operate and are not complicated. Readily available locos and wagons can be used, or, if you are keen on kit- or scratch-building, you could do that too.

Blagdon
The Somerset & Dorset in 4mm scale
by Neil Burgess

During the mid-1990s my railway modelling had reached an impasse. Over the previous 30 years I had built a series of 4mm-scale layouts to OO standards, some of not inconsiderable size, all based on the former Midland Railway lines in the Bristol and Gloucestershire area where I had grown up. Most of these had been fairly conventional in concept and construction, but I had come to the conclusion that all of them, while satisfying in different ways, also had shortcomings that I now wished to transcend in any future piece of modelling. In particular I wanted to try to address the need for reliable and prototypical operation; it was no good producing something that looked nice but was incapable of being operating in a realistic manner, or possibly not working at all!

The need was to get the fundamental philosophy and constructional approach right, not least because I had become convinced that any future project should be built to finescale OO standards. It also seemed important to have a layout that could be completed in a reasonable time. Even if a model railway is never finished, it does seem important that it can be sufficiently complete to look acceptable, while allowing that there are always refinements and developments that can be attempted. An incomplete layout may be a spur to further effort, but if it seems

never to get near to completion – possibly because it cannot be made to work reliably or convincingly – disillusionment sets in.

In writing this I recognise that here is a rationale for the small layout: something that can be used

Above: **This view shows almost all of 'Blagdon', including the sector plate (top left). Notice the space saved by the single-slip point opposite the platform instead of having separate right- and left-hand ones.** *Steve Flint, courtesy of Railway Modeller*

Below: **Plan of 'Blagdon'. The line off to the left is an extension to Weston-super-Mare that was never built, while the line to the right, via the sector plate, is to Binegar. 1 Water tank, 2 PW hut, 3 Station building, 4 Parcels lock-up, 5 Ground frame, 6 Sector plate, 7 Scenic divide (footpath), 8 2-ton crane, 9 Silcock's feed store, 10 Goods lock-up (grounded van body), 11 Loading dock, 12 Blagdon-Burrington road, 13 Storage road behind scenic divide, 14 Allotment**

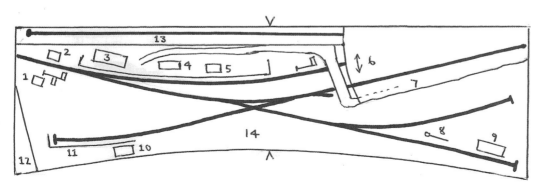

Above: **A lovely shot of a branch goods train. Note the realistic trees.** *Steve Flint, courtesy of Railway Modeller*

to try new approaches, or to develop a modelling philosophy; that can be brought to a satisfying state of completion within a reasonable time; and that can possibly lay the foundations for future modelling projects.

The old Somerset & Dorset Joint line, linking Bournemouth with Bath by way of east Dorset and on over an improbably steep route across the Mendips, has attracted the attention of countless railway enthusiasts, despite closing more than 40 years ago in 1966. Apart from the main line, it had a cluster of branches, the main one being from Evercreech Junction to Highbridge and Burnham-on-Sea, with offshoots from Glastonbury to Wells and Edington Junction to Bridgwater; there were, however, no branches off the Bath Extension north of Evercreech. Undaunted, I invented one that left the main line at Binegar, struck north-west to cross the Bristol to Wells main road, wound its way through Priddy and Charterhouse-on-Mendip and ended in the village of Blagdon. There was, in reality, a railway to Blagdon, but this approached from the west, off the

Great Western's Cheddar Valley line at Congresbur and rejoiced in the title of the Wrington Vale Ligh Railway. Such playing fast and loose with railwa history did not stop there, and I managed to invent whole outline history of the line, including fictitio articles in *The Railway Magazine* for 1955; visitin the area I even half-convinced myself that the lin existed. Though this may seem excessive to some, is important – to me at least – to have some rational for a layout, even if, as with Blagdon, one merel models a small section of the end of the line. All this is very much in the style of that latter-day doye of small layouts, Iain Rice, who has made much this 'concept modelling' in his writings; the approac is more advanced in the United States, but none th worse for that!

The track layout at Blagdon is another borrowin from Iain Rice, being essentially his 'Llanastr Maw concept, though I must admit that at the time I dre it out I was unaware that Iain had managed to hav such an influence. The fact that the fiddle yard within the overall length of the layout helps avoi producing something that is simply too long – a fau that had undermined an earlier attempt. 'Blagdo was also built to be operated from the front. At hom it hardly matters, but it has been interesting to see the difference this makes at the occasional exhibition, where I am out with the spectators; the result seems to be that they are more willing to chat, sometimes at great length and with much interest.

The completed layout measures 2.2 by 0.55 metres – or 7ft 3in by 1ft 10in – and when at home it sits atop a pair of bookcases in my workroom, making rail level about 1.58 metres or 5ft 2in above the floor. This means that one gains a more-or-less prototypical eye-level view, so that it is necessary to peer around structures and landforms in much the same way as one would with a real station. I do think this helps, especially with small layouts; we know they are small, but there's no need to emphasise it by being able to see everything at once. I also made sure that there was almost no straight track on the layout, apart from the siding in front of the feed store. While there are places in Britain where long sections of ruler-straight line exist – the old Bristol & Exeter line from Yatton to Bridgwater and the Great Northern line from Peakirk through Spalding to Boston being cases in point – they are very rare and most lines curve and wind their way through the landscape. British lines are rarely dead level, either; they climb and drop with the contours of the land, so Blagdon has a ruling gradient of 1 in 60, easing to level through the platform. With fairly easy-running wagons this makes shunting interesting to say the least; it is not unknown to put something 'on the ground' when it runs away through the trap points at the lower end of the loop.

'Blagdon' has achieved the aims I set for it and has been an enduring source of interest to build and operate. Even two-day stints at several exhibitions have been enjoyable, if tiring, experiences. So the Somerset & Dorset lives on, albeit in 4mm scale.

Lane End
The North Staffordshire in 7mm scale
by Neil Burgess

I came upon modelling the North Staffordshire Railway almost by accident. My late father-in-law, Eric Mullineux, was the son of a former North Staffordshire employee, who had started with the company around the time of the Great War. Eric himself had served an engineering apprenticeship at the Castle Locomotive Works of W. G. Bagnall in Stafford just after the Second World War, so had an appreciation of what goes into building locomotives. In retirement, he started modelling the NSR, first in 2mm scale, then in 7mm. Finding no kits available at the time, he commissioned Rod Neep to design some for locomotives, carriages and wagons, and had a number etched in 2mm, 4mm and 7mm scales. Sadly, Eric died before his project came to fruition and I inherited what he had managed to put together so far.

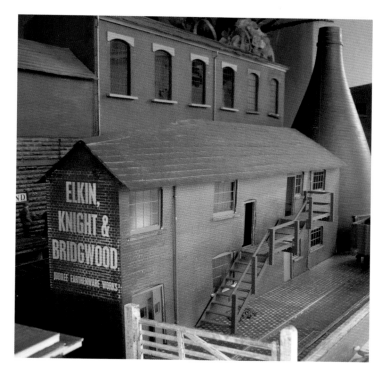

Above: **A view showing the excellent buildings, especially the kiln.** *Neil Burgess*

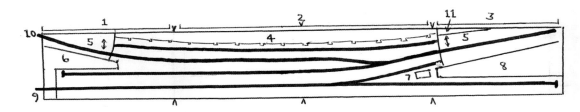

Plan of the scenic section of 'Lane End'. 1 Backscene: Enoch Clowes Colour Works, 2 Backscene: half-relief buildings of Railway Street, 3 Backscene: Bourne Memorial Primitive Methodist Chapel, 4 Retaining wall, 5 Sector plates, 6 Holland & Birch Engineering Works, 7 Signal frame, 8 Elkin, Knight & Bridgwood Pottery Works, 9 Line to Longton Hall Colliery and Lower Normacot Wharf, 10 Line to Longton and Stoke-Derby main line, 11 End of station platform

Having spent 49 years modelling in 4mm scale, it took a bit of time to get the measure of 7mm. Obviously things are bigger – even small locomotives seem huge – but it takes time to realise just how much the increased size affects the way one thinks of what can – and cannot – be done. Even a simple matter like a pair of crossovers and a run-round loop grew to unimagined dimensions, and this affected what sort of layout might be possible.

It was while trying to puzzle out what I might do that I read Gordon Gravett's two-volume *7mm Modelling* (Wild Swan Publications, 1996 and 2000). The second book contained a plan for a small portable layout where running-round was effected not by pointwork but a train turntable, hidden from view behind industrial buildings. Not being one to pass up a good idea, I seized upon and used it as the basis of a small terminal station set in a deeply industrial part of Stoke-on-Trent. Having already rewritten the history of the Somerset & Dorset line for my 'Blagdon' layout, I proceeded to do the same with the North Staffordshire, and in particular the Longton, Adderley Green & Bucknall Railway, a goods-only line around the Longton area of the Potteries, not far from where my wife and I had lived years before. Homage was duly paid to Arnold Bennett, the novelist of the Potteries, by naming the station 'Lane End', his pseudonym for Longton.

'Lane End' needed not only to be portable but capable of being stored in a space measuring 85 by 45 centimetres (33½ by 17¾ inches), which dictated the size of each section, and also to be capable of having the sections stacked box-like one on top of the other. The Gravett plan suggested that pairs of sections could be hinged to fold one on top of the other, with flaps dropping down in the front of each section when the layout was set up. This has been more or less adopted, though the pairs of sections aren't hinged together and the whole layout stacks into a space 3ft 9in high. When erected the five sections produce an overall length of 4.25 by 0.45 metres (virtually 14 feet by 1ft 6in), not that big for a 7mm-scale layout it equates to 8 feet by 10¼ inches in 4mm scale which seems even more compact!

Certain other ideas were built into Lane End not least to exploit the advantages that modelling urban areas has for people without much space. Urban railways tend to be constrained by retaining walls, thread under bridges and appear and disappear behind buildings, which, because they too are short of room, are built vertically rather than allowed to spread horizontally. This provides ample scenic breaks behind which to lose trains without having to resort to hackneyed devices like the tunnel suddenly rising up out of a flat plain. It was important to emphasise the vertical dimension altogether, since this tends to confirm the sense of a train moving through a townscape rather than dominating its surroundings. Avoiding dead straight track and introducing a 1 in 40 gradient down the branch to Longton Hall colliery and the brickworks also help move away from the 'flat earth' approach.

'Lane End' is set in 1912. Pre-Grouping modelling offers other advantages to modellers short of room, not least that engines tended to be smaller and trains shorter and composed of more compact vehicles than was the case after 1923. The

A view showing the retaining wall and a lovely loco not often seen modelled. *Neil Burgess*

North Staffordshire was very much a 'tank engine' railway, some very small by modern standards. Most NSR branches seem to have been operated using four-coach sets of four- or six-wheeled coaches; with a small 2-4-0 tank, these amount to about 4 feet at most, and three coaches and a 2-4-2 tank to about a yard. Goods wagons also tended to be smaller than those produced after 1923, certainly the common types of minerals, opens and covered vans. Taking these factors together allows a compact layout that can still be interesting to operate and conveys the feel of an urban line hemmed in by buildings and civil engineering.

Some further subterfuges have been resorted to in order to gain greatest advantage from the small space. The station is more hinted at than modelled in full, the narrow platform tapering away to almost nothing with only the outer end properly visible. It is actually hidden behind a 'pot bank' and is at the foot of a retaining wall surmounted by a Primitive Methodist chapel, both distracting the viewer's attention from its sparseness. At the opposite end the passenger line disappears behind the premises of Messrs Holland & Birch, wagon repairers and general engineers, while in front of their works the goods line to Longton Hall Colliery and Lower Normacot Wharf drops down its fearsome gradient – wagons really run away on 1 in 40! Instead of pairs of points to make crossovers at either end of the run-round loop, two hidden sector plates are used to save space and suggest that the track formation is actually much larger than in reality.

As a first essay in 7mm scale, 'Lane End' has taught me a good deal and there may be more to learn before it is completed. It's just a pity that Eric isn't here to see what he started.

Lower Normacot Wharf
Another North Staffordshire project in 7mm scale
by Neil Burgess

The North Staffordshire Railway was a small company by British standards, but it was nevertheless the third largest railway owner of canals. This was a legacy of the Industrial Revolution and

'Lower Normacot Wharf' is an attempt to embody some of this interrelationship between the North Staffordshire and its canals. Normacot is a real place in the Potteries and for many years was served by a station on the Stoke-Derby line but this model is sited at the opposite end of the district down on the edge of Dresden and Florence. The latter district was named after a colliery, once owned by the Duke of Sutherland and in turn named after one of his daughters. The ducal seat

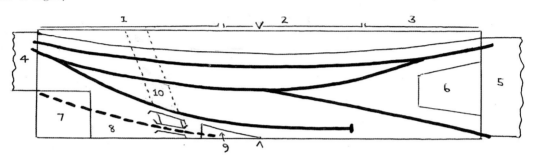

Plan of 'Lower Normacot Wharf', modelled, like 'Lane End', in 1912. 1 Backscene: Sherratt & Smith Colour Works and Hollick, Moreton & Page Joinery Works, 2 Backscene: Nowell, Gosling & Stubbs Timber Merchants, 3 Backscene: Holland & Birch Engineers, 4 Pull-out platform for sector plate; line to Trentham, 5 Pull-out platform for sector plate lines to Lane End and Longton Hall Colliery (upper) and Florence Colliery (lower), 6 Railway and Canal Office, 7 Loading shed over basin, 8 Canal basin (Trent & Mersey Navigation), 9 Coal chutes, 10 Canal under railway

the transport network that had both created the pottery industry and Stoke-on-Trent. Before the railways arrived on the scene in the 1840s there already existed a network of canals, of which the Trent & Mersey Navigation, linking those two major river systems, was the most significant. Whereas other railway companies often acquired canals in order to put them out of business or convert them to railways, the North Staffordshire saw them as a complementary means of transport and ran them accordingly. Indeed, many of the pot banks were connected to the canals rather than the railways, so integration made good commercial sense.

Right and opposite: **Two views showing 'Lower Normacot Wharf' under construction. Unintentionally, Neil has shown us another site for a layout, if the design of your house permits it, namely the landing.** *Both Neil Burgess*

of Trentham Hall was situated near the Trent & Mersey Navigation and I have assumed that a branch canal was built from Trentham to carry

oal from Florence and Longton Hall collieries. The railway part of the layout is assumed to be a branch from Lane End to the wharf, which is a transhipment point for coal, lime and timber.

The first challenge presented by 'Lower Normacot Wharf' was to build a convincing layout in a very small space for 7mm scale. The scenic section measures just 6ft 6in by 1ft 8in (2 by 0.51 metres), which on a 4mm scale model is the equivalent of 3ft 8in by 1 foot. Bearing in mind that three average 7mm scale wagons from the pre-Grouping era take up around 15 inches, this is very much minimal-space modelling!

I have long been fascinated by old, small industrial sites, the sorts of places that were once very common all over Britain, but which have long disappeared under new housing developments, business parks and other kinds of gin palaces. Many of these places were poorly recorded; they were neither visually attractive nor prestigious as centres of industry, but from time to time someone with a camera did discover and photograph them. Trawling through publications like Railway Bylines,

the 'Real Atmosphere' sections of Model Railway Journal and a host of other sources can often reveal all kinds of fascinating buildings. Some years ago Railway Bylines ran a photographic feature on Leicester West Bridge, the inner terminus of the Leicester & Swannington Railway, and Gerry Beal's book on the Weymouth Harbour Tramway (Wild Swan, 2001) yielded some very interesting views of a harbourside timber yard. However, a couple of buildings, including the wharf office, have been lifted from streets very close to my home, so it's important not to neglect the inspiration on your doorstep. There are also a fair number of books on the canals of Staffordshire and I look forward to building a model of the narrow boat Farmer's Friend, which carried lime from Froghall Wharf on the Cauldon Canal (near the present terminus of the Churnet Valley Railway) to the Potteries; I shall also include a model of the splendidly moustachioed Primrose Thorley, partner in Thorley & Bowers, lime burners of Froghall and owners of this and several other boats.

Above: **I have used this photo for one purpose only – to show the ingenious method of supporting the cassettes, which Neil calls 'pull-out platforms'.** *Neil Burgess*

The West Bridge photos showed track running in granite setts, which offers an interesting change from the everyday cross-sleepered version. Track does need hand-building for a layout like this, since no one is realistically going to offer pointwork to fit the kinds of eccentric patterns required. It's a good few years since I built any pointwork for myself and that was in 4mm scale, but I'm reasonably confident that taking things slowly and carefully should avoid the more obvious problems. Indeed, building your own track fits in well with a small layout like this – it's not as if you need miles of it, so you can achieve a reasonable result fairly soon.

The other question raised by 'Lower Normacot Wharf' was how to provide fiddle yards. The conventional wisdom says these need to be built as extra baseboards, with some kind of surface on which either permanent sidings or else removable cassettes can sit. It occurred to me that on a model this small, where the greatest length of train would be around 2ft 6in, it might be possible to build pull-out platforms on which to stand the cassettes, rather like the kinds of additional work surfaces found in some modern kitchens ('fully fitted kitchen' sounds to me like it should be vacuum braked throughout). Purveyors of bits for baseboard construction supply steel drawer runners with ball-bearing sliders and other refinements, so these have been used to produce the pull-out sections. It is important to allow enough clearance between the runners and the underside of the track bases to enable point controls and wiring to be fitted in, but beyond this it all seems reasonably straightforward.

'Lower Normacot Wharf' is at present very much 'work in progress', but hopefully this sort of small-scale project might inspire others to 'have a go', particularly if this is a first attempt to model in a different scale; or even to try scratch-building altogether. I think it's sufficiently challenging to make the attempt worthwhile – it's a bit self defeating if it's too easy; or at least that's what I think most of the time. Once built, or at least operable, it should provide enough challenge there to retain interest too.

Vine Street Yard
American ¼in to 1 foot scale
by Marshall Vine

'Vine Street Yard' was built to see just how small, workable, interesting O gauge layout could be bearing in mind the large size of American freight cars. At only slightly over 7 feet long, including the sector table, which also serves as a fiddle yard, it still allows sensible switching operations to a number of different industries. It is set in the 1940s/1950s era, when steam and diesel locos could be seen together, and before the larger modern rolling stock came on the scene. Its location is supposedly Chicago, where Vine Street actually exists at the very end of the Kingsbury branch, although there is no actual yard there.

The layout is only made possible because of two important features: the use of Atlas 2-foot-radius points, and the sector table, which replaces several points and thus saves space. The use of such a small radius in O gauge is not a problem since the rolling stock (with one small exception) is all bogie vehicles and can easily cope with the sharp curves. (In fact, such sharp curves were not unknown in some prototype situations in the States!) One limiting factor is that only the smaller locomotives can be used, although this too is only prototypical since any loco used in a similar full-sized yard would of necessity be small.

Unfortunately, the points used are no longer available. The current Atlas range includes only large-radius points, so the old ones must now be found on the second-hand market.

The sector table is the real secret to the layout's operation. From the plan it can be seen that it replaces two further points, forms the end of the run-round loop, and even connects with another siding that is otherwise totally unconnected with the rest of the layout. To disguise this arrangement an unpowered track crosses the layout on a large girder bridge, backed up by a factory flat under which three of the tracks disappear. When the layout is on display, this track is usually home to a much larger locomotive, which, while much too large to run on the layout, adds a bit more interest. The sector table is hidden from the front by a continuation of the factory back scene, which also provides another destination for freight traffic.

The background buildings, which completely surround the layout, are all from a highly recommended American source, Westport Model Works. They are printed on card in a modular arrangement so can be extended as required by just adding more sheets. Those used on 'Vine Street Yard' are all from two basic buildings in the range. They can be much more detailed if required, with opening windows, etc, but as part of the idea of building the layout was to see just how easily a reasonable result could be obtained, the sheets were used just as they came, except that one was reversed in the computer to make a set of steps go the other way. The printed sheets are mounted on foamboard for lightness, apart from those hiding the sector table where, as a bit more strength was required, plywood was used. One building has a track going into it, protected by a 'roller shutter' door. This is a real hi-tech piece of equipment, being operated by pulling a string behind the scenes!

Plan of 'Vine Street Yard'. 1 Water tower, 2 Yard tower, 3 Unpowered track on girder bridge, 4 Sector table

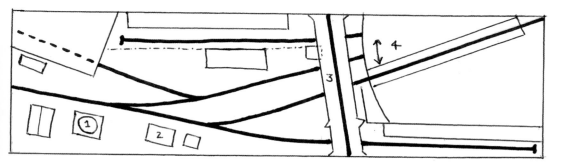

There is little room on such a small layout for large three-dimensional buildings, but room has been found for a small yard tower and a water tower. To keep faith with the original idea of an easy-build layout, both of these are basic plastic kits from the Lionel 'Hi-rail' range. In addition, as most railroad yards seem to collect lots of odd, often decrepit sheds, 'Vine Street Yard' is no exception. The three in front of the wire fence are all from a very useful plastic kit of three sheds by Bachmann. They are already moulded to look as though they are well past their sell-by date

so, with careful painting, can really add character to a scene.

The rolling stock is a real mixture, with just about every manufacturer of both ready-to-run and kits represented. Most cars are 40-foot boxcars, of different types to add some variety, although other types of car do appear. The piece of equipment that causes most interest is the little orange car seen in the centre of the close-up photo. It is a scale test car, used for checking the accuracy of weigh bridges. Since there are special rules governing their use, it can makes switching (shunting) much more complicated. Due to the small size of the layout, only two or three cars can be moved at a time. The loop will hold two 40-foot cars while the sector table is long enough for two cars and a small engine.

The locomotives are as varied as the cars, again ranging through many manufacturers. Both small diesel and steam types are used, but unfortunately models of small steam locos are a bit thin on the ground. Consequently modeller's licence has been taken and several of the small 'geared' locomotives such as 'Shay' and 'Climax', more usually associated with backwoods logging operations, are often used. These locos usually generate quite a bit of interest from the public as they are generally not well known over here. A large locomotive is always displayed on the bridge, helping to disguise the yard exit. It can range from a large 0-8-8-0 'camelback' shown in the photograph, to an unpowered 2-10-2, made from doctored plastic kit solely as part of the scenery. However, the well-known

Above: **The whole of 'Vine Street Yard' at an exhibition, showing how compact it is. Note the large loco on the bridge.** *Marshall Vine*

Below: **A close-up view of 'Vine Street Yard' showing the scenic detail around the brown shed, which really brings the scene to life.** *Marshall Vine*

Big Boy' 4-8-8-4 cannot be used as, believe it or not, it is a foot longer than the width of the layout!

The electrics can be quickly summed up in one word: simple. There is just the one controller as the layout is much too small for anything more complicated. There is really only room for only one locomotive to be used at a time anyway, although a couple of others can be isolated at different places if required. A pelmet with a couple of small fluorescent tubes lights the layout, often very necessary as a surprising number of exhibition halls are somewhat dimly lit.

The layout was always designed to be exhibited, to show that an O-gauge layout need be neither large nor difficult to build, yet still offer interesting operation. In fact, its small size actually adds to its interest for the operators. It is only too easy to get stuck while moving cars around such a restricted space if movements are not thought out well in advance. It is not operated to any sequence, but at the whim of the operator.

So this is 'Vine Street Yard' – basic, small and simple. When describing a layout, the reader is often taken on an imaginary ride round it, while the main features are described. With 'Vine Street Yard' this is not necessary. Being so small, it could all be seen by simply standing on an imaginary packing case somewhere in the middle!

Finally, it is worth bearing in mind that although the present layout follows an American theme, only the replacement of a couple of buildings would be required to move it somewhere else. Small, four-wheel British or continental stock would look just as much at home as the larger American types, as the actual track plan and most of the scenery are universal.

Vine Creek Mine
American ¼in to 1 foot scale
by Marshall Vine

This little layout, really only a working diorama, came about by accident! A larger 0n30 layout was planned when the Wealden Railway Group Layout Competition came on the scene. This group specialises in small layouts and the challenge was to produce a layout in a space of 1 metre by 1 foot! No real problem in 2mm scale perhaps, but how about 7mm or, to be more correct, the American 0n30 scale of quarter-inch to the foot?

Several traditional back-of-envelope sketches showed that a workable yet credible track plan was possible. The proposed layout was set in Colorado (where else!), so little horizontal space was needed for scenery, vertical rock faces being the order of the day. To give this more emphasis, the actual baseboard was set up 4½ inches on a deep box, which meant that the scenery could dip well below track level. This makes the layout higher than it is wide, but helps to give the impression that the track runs along a rocky shelf.

The track is Peco 16.5 narrow gauge, glued direct to the board. It was not raised as it was intended that the track should look thoroughly neglected, as though it was slowly sinking into the ground. Ballast is therefore rather sparse, while lumps of grass were planted liberally between the rails.

For such a small layout the wiring is surprisingly complex, arranged for two controllers. This was done so that a sound-equipped engine – these are very common now in the States – could be left on a still live section quietly talking to itself while another moved by it. Several Kaydee electromagnetic uncouplers in the usual places allow more or less hands-free operation.

There is space for only a few buildings, really only the mine, depot and loco shed. The mine is a stock model from the Walther's catalogue. It is an impressive model with lots of character, but I do rather doubt its authenticity! Not obvious from the catalogue was the fact that it is made of some sort of ceramic material, so modifying it to fit a working ore chute was a bit traumatic, but after weathering to tone down the bright colours it fits in very well. The loco shed is a 'Smokey Bottom' resin kit but with doors added, while the depot building is actually a laser-cut kit for a yard office, but even that had to be reduced in size! Of the only other structures, the water tower and coal stage were scratch built, while the privy is another laser wood kit.

The rock faces are a prominent part of the layout, and most are vacuum-moulded sheets from Finishing Touches of Leicester. Their big advantage

Above: 'Vine Creek Mine': the whole layout at Tywyn MRC's exhibition. *David Mitchell*

Below: A close-up of the mine that gives the layout its name. *Marshall Vine*

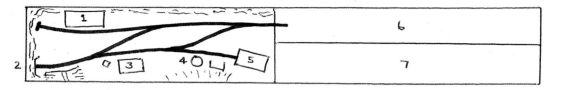

Plan of 'Vine Creek Mine'. 1 Mine, 2 Mouth of 'unsafe' tunnel, 3 Depot building, 4 Water tower and coal stage, 5 Loco shed, 6 Fiddle yard, 7 Display area

s lightness, saving a lot of weight over rocks made from plaster. They don't look bad in their natural state, but a coat of various shades of texture paint and a bit of greenery on the ledges really transforms them. Most of this vegetation, particularly the lumps of grass, are from International Models. These clumps are very easy to use: just peel them off the backing sheet and stick them down with a blob of white glue. They are really effective and are used all over the layout, even between the rails.

At one end of the layout an 'unsafe' tunnel makes it appear that the line once carried on. A lot of time was taken to deepen the half-inch or so of tunnel by painting a view looking through it. This worked very well, but is almost invisible to the spectators! It may well disappear anyway as it is proposed to reinstate through traffic in the near future.

As with most layouts, particularly the smallest, there are far too many locomotives. The Bachmann On30 range is well represented, but there are several more unusual ones, mainly resin kits from the USA. Several others are from the Backwoods Miniatures range of kits, while the vertical-boiler loco from Smallbrook Works on the Isle of Wight is just the sort of thing a backwoods blacksmith might have made out of bits and pieces! One particularly interesting loco is an American resin kit for an early 'Climax' loco, just a bit out of the ordinary.

Rolling stock is equally varied, with most On30 manufacturers represented, again including some from the USA. Apart from the ready-to-run examples, there are kits in wood, metal, resin and plastic. There are even a couple of scratch-built items. As it is a very small layout, only the smaller items can be used. The Chivers Finelines kits are particularly useful as they are very much smaller

than the standard Bachmann cars, while you have all the fun of making them!

Operation of the layout is very casual, a polite way of saying that the operator does what he likes! There is no fixed pattern except that every so often some suitable cars are put into the mine spur for loading. Some trains just come in and reverse, as it is supposed that a logging line branches off just off scene beyond the engine shed. The overall track plan is therefore assumed to be Y-shaped, which gives an excuse for a wider variety of trains.

And that's about it – a lot of words about 3 square feet and a bit. Not that it will stay that way, as a new board of the same size is already under way. This will extend the main line over the creek that gives the mine its name, while the previously only imagined junction will actually exist. As already mentioned, there is even talk of clearing the tunnel rock fall and reopening the line through it. We'll just have to wait and see.

Walker Marine
by Neil Ripley

Just because a layout is restricted by limitations of space doesn't necessarily mean that it cannot still be based upon, or at least inspired by, a real location. Indeed, many of the award winning layouts and plans conceived by East Yorkshire-based modeller Neil Ripley were inspired by period photographs of off-the-beaten-track prototypes, the likes of industrial, dockland and light railway locations in particular, suiting his approach to small layout design, as well as making for visually and scenically interesting models.

One of Neil's earliest exhibition layouts, 'Walker Marine' actually had a surprisingly long gestation period prior to seeing the light of day, with the gritty reality of Ian S. Carr's evocative 1960s photographs of the shipyard railways and their surroundings in Sunderland providing initial inspiration in his late teens. Neil spent a further decade researching the subject of the shipyards and their rail systems, whilst dabbling with various design concepts both in paper form and as 3D mock-ups of layouts based around parts of the 'Doxford Shipyard' system before opportunity, improvements in modelling skills level and availability of suitable stock made the creation of a layout based on that research actually feasible.

It is certainly not a micro-scheme per se; considering all that is included, it is surprising that scenically the layout still only occupies a space some 6 feet long by 2ft 3in deep, flanked by an additional 2 feet at either end for fiddle yards. With the best will in the world the area available could in no way practically and convincingly depict the slipways and heavy engineering side of such a works. Neil successfully got around this by depicting other parts of the works, together with the exchange loop and passing British Railways line in a multi-level format. It has an unusual form of presentation, in that the model was deliberately built with the highest levels towards the front so as to give the viewer the impression of looking down across the works and towards the river. It mirrors the viewpoints depicted in many of those Ian S. Carr photographs that inspired the model in the first place. The resultant model, built in conjunction with Malcolm Baker and Colin Stark (and with the assistance of others), though in no way intended to be an accurate depiction of any part of the 'Doxford' system, does include enough of the look of the prototype to capture the spirit and atmosphere of it, and thus is instantly recognisable to anyone familiar with it.

From the initial design stages of the model due consideration was given to how this unusual model would be constructed, transported and stored, particularly as some elements of the scenic work would be relatively fragile; yet the model as a whole would have to be easily portable and survive the rigours of travelling and handling associated with life on the exhibition circuit. As such the model consisted of three 'open frame' baseboards built in softwood and ply. They were arranged as a pair of 4-foot-long boards with an additional 2-foot one to make up the length, each having integral back/front scenes and folding legs to speed up the processes of erection and dismantling. The scenic section is framed by a folding fascia/lighting unit when in use. Due to the multiple-track-level design, and therefore the depth and weight of the supporting structure, it was impractical to transport the main pair of boards bolted face-to-face, as had been done with some previous layouts. Therefore each has a complete 'box cover' constructed of thin ply, which allows the boards to stack as well as providing protection for the vulnerable scenery and track ends in both transportation and storage. With such thought put into the design and protection of the model, it is not surprising that the model could be erected or dismantled in less than 30 minutes.

Although it was certainly desirable to have trackwork of a realistic appearance on the layout the need for both reliability and durability over the long term was also taken into account. Therefore based on prior experience, all turnouts were hand-built and of copper-clad construction. This was combined with commercially available EM-gauge flexible track from SMP, and all was laid upon a base of cork floor tiles. This combination has proved to stand up to the rigours of intensive exhibition usage very well, the only non-electrical problem encountered being related to broken tie bars or over-generous application of paint or glue! The same premise of keeping to simple but robust methods was carried over to the electrical systems. Here the

Neil Ripley's multi-level 'Walker Marine' layout, unusually seen here from the *rear*.

These two photos just ooze atmosphere. If you did not know they were of a model, you would think it was the 'real thing'. This is mainly due to Neil Ripley's superb layout design skills. *Both Steve Flint, courtesy of Railway Modeller*

control system effectively mirrors the model's 'dual layout' design with electrically separate systems and independent control panels for the upper and lower levels. Stock is transferred between the two levels via a single-track sector plate, which is energised by whichever level track it is aligned with.

The unusual 'back to front' design of the layout effectively ruled out the blanket use of any simple form of manual point operation. Therefore, in the locations where manual control is prevented, operation is provided through Seep motors, acting upon separate microswitches to alter the polarity of the respective point. Conventional control was the order of the day here, via a set of hand-held units. DCC might have been considered a useful alternative if the layout had been built many years later. However, even then, the diminutive size of some of the locomotives used might have called for some degree of ingenuity to be employed in fitting the decoders.

It is the structures and scenery that give the model much of its visual presence. As such it comes as no surprise to find that both were thoroughly researched, both through study of period photographs and a visit to the area, to ensure that the 'look' of the model reflected that of the area. Neil admits that, unlike previous models, which endeavoured to accurately recreate a prototype location and therefore required faithful reproductions of specific structures, the less regimented nature of the prototype here and the thinking behind this model as that of a 'typical' rather than 'specific' location did allow for a more relaxed approach. The aim was to capture the atmosphere of the area, representing the building types, styles and materials rather than any one particular prototype. Hence the need to get the colours and ageing finishes of the buildings right through proper research.

Being representative of a large industrial complex, the mixture of architectural styles and material is more indicative of long-term development of the site, where a building's construction and appearance is more likely to reflect its intended usage and period of construction rather than any specific local architectural traits. Therefore, based on guidance notes from site research, models were selected and built to suit their specific layout locations, based mainly on conversions of plastic structure kits intended for the American or European markets. Some are now so heavily modified, detailed and weathered, and so removed from their origins, that they are often taken for scratch-built. In addition there are several outbuildings, factory chimneys, roof ventilators and a whole array of scratch-built overhead pipework to bring the scene to life.

All this is enhanced by a few cameo scenes of workers going about their business among the road vehicles, piles of material, scrap, signalling equipment, animals and other incidental details, added to interest the spectator and create scenes reminiscent of those period photographs that inspired the model in the first place.

The selection of locomotives and rolling stock was always quite varied, but all of which reflected typical examples that could have been seen either in industry or on British Railways metals in the region in which the model was set in the early part of the 1960s. The locomotives on the industrial side almost exclusively originated as kits, though not always built as the manufacturer intended, whereas several of the British Railways locomotives featured modified and detailed proprietary bodies mounted upon heavily modified or replacement etched brass chassis kits. All were built to EM-gauge standards. A two-car Metro-Cammell DMU modified from a Lima model was sufficient to handle the passenger workings. Freight and parcels traffic called upon examples of 'J72', 'J94' and 'V3' 2-6-2 tank locomotives, 204hp DM and 350hp DE shunters, and a BR/Sulzer Type 2 Bo-Bo. These were based upon examples allocated to or operating in the region. Examples of the classic 'J27' 0-6-0 or Clayton centre-cab diesel would really have been more typical and desirable motive power for such as the coal train, but for the restrictions of practicality imposed by the length of the fiddle yards.

As for the industrial fleet, Neil initially tried not to emulate the usual model railway pitfall of having one example of everything, going more for the prototype practice of 'batch'-purchasing clearly reflected in the illustrations of fleets of such large industries. As such he started out with a fleet made up of pairs or more of less similar locomotives. Naturally these were headed by a brace of Doxford 4-ton crane locomotives built from Backwoods Miniatures kits supported initially by a fleet of ready-to-run-based 'Austerity' 0-6-0STs. However, retirement of older, life-expired or less detailed examples in favour of newer kit-built models meant that over the lifespan of the layout the fleet of industrial locomotives did start to degenerate into a bit of a mixed bunch, admittedly all resplendent in the company's blue/black livery with straw lining. The Doxford crane locomotives were latterly supported by a similarly equipped Neilson Crane Tank, together with conventional RSH, Andrew Barclay, Black Hawthorne and Peckett saddle tanks, and, with a nod toward modernisation, a pair of Yorkshire Engine Co 0-4-0 diesel shunters based on a design supplied to the Port of London Authority (converted from DJH BR Class 02 kits).

The rolling stock, like the locomotives, had the odd detailed item of ready-to-run origin, but was for the most part based upon plastic or white metal kits, though often with replacement under-frame detail, or indeed with modifications to construct examples or variations not available straight from the kits. As with the locomotives, all were finished with a patina of weathering, texturing and distressing to reflect the materials and usage of the particular prototype being modelled, together with, in some cases, loads, sheeting or packing materials added to complete the effect.

'Walker Marine' remained a popular layout throughout its ten years on the exhibition circuit, visiting shows both in the UK and in Europe. Indeed, the layout is still often mentioned as the inspiration for several others. However, the story doesn't quite finish with retirement, as subsequent to its final show the model was sold and shipped to a new home in California! This was not for a quiet retirement as a home layout, as one might have imagined, as its keen new owner has ideas for further development within the original premise of the model and intends to put it back on the exhibition circuit at some point, although admittedly several thousand miles from where it started out!

Carlton Metals
by Neil Ripley

Due to the success of Neil Ripley's tribute to the North East shipbuilding industry, which proved particularly popular on the exhibition circuit, together with his involvement in other projects, it was a good few years before he actually took any of his many designs further than the sketch pad and built another layout. However, the chance to enter a competition to design and construct a fully operational layout in a maximum area of 4½ square feet prompted him to come up with 'Carlton Metals'. This late-1960s depiction of the yard of a Midlands light engineering company that has diversified into dealing with scrap metal (including breaking railway rolling stock) had the additional scenic twist of being set in the depths of a snowy winter.

As with 'Walker Marine', pre-constructional planning and a degree of forethought were paramount in ensuring that the finished model would not only be visually pleasing but could also be constructed quickly and without any major problems, and that it would be easy to erect and dismantle, durable, and as fault-free as possible in operation.

With the entire model occupying a space just 4ft 6in long by 1 foot wide, the model needed only a single baseboard of those dimensions. A 2-by-1-inch PSE softwood frame of those exterior dimensions topped with 9mm MDF was sufficient, supported by a pair of 3ft 6in softwood leg frames stabilised by a bolt-on crossbar 1 foot from ground level. Though very simple, the resultant substructure proved very stable when erected, resembling a school desk. For ease of transport the scenic board had an overall hardboard cover and the support frame and legs were designed to easily bolt together into one practical and easy-to-carry unit, making the whole model as small and practical as possible, so as to facilitate easy transport with two operators and stock, etc, in a small hatchback car.

Although built this time to the more trade-supported OO (16.5mm) gauge, the trackwork was again hand-built copper-clad-based pointwork combined with SMP flexible trackwork. However, a short diamond crossing from the Peco code 75 range was also added to the mix in order to simplify the wiring and speed up construction. The resultant combination was trackwork all laid with care on a base of cork floor tiles, with thought to the positioning of track joints and the minimum radii. This, combined with manual point operation via under-board rodding activated by way of SPDT side switches (which also change the polarity of the frogs), made for durable and reliable trackwork and therefore more reliable operation of stock. In fact, Neil reports that the only real issues with the trackwork were caused by his own overzealous applications of paint and snow! Point control aside, the only additional switches required were those providing isolation at three chosen locations, as the size of the model, track layout and indeed prototype depicted dictated that, for most aspects of operation, there was a requirement for a single locomotive only. This meant that the layout could be wired for very simple operation.

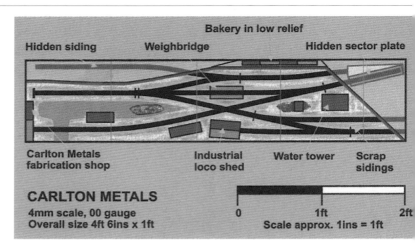

Courtesy of Railway Modell..

Looking at the photos of this unusual model, it is not hard to guess that the scenics were an important consideration right from the initial design stage, with many rough thumbnail sketches and full-size mock-ups with boxes and card to represent features employed during the finalisation of the design. The visual scene is 'enclosed' by the use of retaining walls and overbridges built from Wills materials over plywood supports. These not only provide the scenic breaks for the hidden fiddle yard areas but also give the scene a degree of height to help offset the lack of depth. This was particularly needed in this case as the majority of the width was taken up with a significant amount of trackwork. The few other structures on the model were either plywood shells clad in the appropriate finish of Plasticard or modified or detailed commercially available kits in either plastic or cast plaster. However, like the chapel kit that was used for the basis of the industrial engine shed, the kits were not necessarily used as the manufacturer intended. Further detailing items and scrap vehicles were from the Knightwing and MSE ranges, or the proverbial scrapbox. Each of the items was subjected to a degree of experimentation, being tried out in numerous locations, often several times, until the builder was happy with the composition before gluing them in place.

The few 'serviceable' period road vehicles are, with the exception of the bus, all kit-built items. Neil's initial intention was to install overhead lines and an example of a Nottingham trolleybus on the roadway scene. However, the timely and apt release of a well-detailed model of a Leyland double-decker in Nottingham

Above: **A close-up view of 'Carlton Metals' – note the detail.** *Steve Flin. courtesy of Railway Modeller*

ove: **An overall view of 'Carlton Metals'. The slight snow ~ering is very effective and has been exceptionally well ~e in my view.** *Steve Flint, courtesy of Railway Modeller*

~ty Transport livery complete with 'Carlton' ~te destination was too good an opportunity to ~ss.

The remainder of the scenic detailing consisted ~inly of undergrowth and bushes created from ~oodland Scenics or Anita Decor products. Once ~ the scenics were installed, the structures and ~tails were weathered to suit to give a degree ~ atmosphere to the model, and better depict a ~dy and overgrown industrial yard. However, ~il admits that although he was pleased with ~e scenically finished model, by this stage his ~ventive mind was still at work.

Inspired by others' efforts in creating layouts ~picting seasons and conditions other than ~ernal' summertime, Neil began experimenting ~th a Woodland Scenics product rather ~scriptively described as 'Snow' on the already ~enically complete layout. While the product was ~und to be highly capable of creating effective ~ep drifts, its fine powdery nature was also a boon ~r convincingly representing a light dusting of ~ow. Such a light covering would also allow the

previous scenic work to be seen as well. What you see in the photographs is Neil's attempt to depict a scene where, in spite of the industrial location and weak winter sunshine, remnants of a heavy snowfall a few days earlier are still evident, aided perhaps by the low temperatures and occasional light flurry. Neil completed the layout's scenics over Christmas 2001, his inspiration for the scenario being the prevailing conditions at that time – research was just a matter of opening the curtains! The snow was fixed using either diluted PVA or unscented hairspray, dependant on the required thickness and location. To complete the scene, additional frosting on walls and sleepers was added by dry-brushing white acrylic paint.

The wintry weathering using snow and paint detailing was also carried over to the rolling stock, over and above the usual workaday finishes. The stock itself was a combination of vehicles of both ready-to-run and kit origin, and consisted of a handful of British Railways and ex-company vans and opens for the traffic to the engineering side, with a decent rake of well-weathered steel mineral wagons for handling outward scrap metals destined for the furnaces of South Yorkshire. Interspersed with this, sporting P-numbers, condemned markings and the sort of weathering that must have had the Barwell staff shaking their heads, were several Bachmann wooden open wagons representing life-expired cast-offs from the local coal industry making their final journey. Likewise it wasn't unknown for the odd small steam locomotive sporting no rods and similar markings to make an appearance.

Handling all this inbound and outbound traffic were examples of Colwick-allocated 200hp and 350hp diesel shunters based on detailed Bachmann models. The 350hp was actually modified and renumbered to represent one of the Blackstone-engined examples, later identified as Class 10.

The company itself used a pensionable Planet 0 4-0 diesel-mechanical from an earlier decade (Roxey Mouldings white metal kit) for interna movements in the yard.

The unusual and somewhat experimenta wintry finish to both layout and stock attracte much comment when the layout was first unveile in 2002, and, much to Neil's surprise, the mode was awarded first place over some other very fin examples. So, all in all, the layout was a succes its compact nature as well as the unusual scenic garnering much praise in the short time that Nei exhibited it before selling it on to make way fo other projects.

St Minions
by Neil Ripley

Now, as a rule, Neil Ripley tends to follow the wise philosophy of designing the layout as a whole first to fit in an area of a particular size, then drawing it out full size and experimenting to see what gives the best visual balance before commencing on any form of construction. He does this because sometimes the appearance and operation of a model can be compromised for the sake of saving a couple of inches when the design and scenics have been made to 'fit' a particularly rigid area. However, 'St Minions' goes against Neil's usual school of thinking in that the baseboard was donated and existed long before the design and the subsequent layout built upon it were even considered.

Neil says that, in spite of his experience in the field, this layout's design was particularly challenging to get right both in aesthetics and operation, as the scenic area is only some 2ft 6in long! Added to which, the baseboard is of irregular frontage, stretching from a width of 18 inches at one end to just 12 at the other, making the whole scenic area tiny compared with even the smallest of the previous layouts. However, with careful thought to both design and presentation, a convincing section of a Cornish branch line complete with passenger halt and part of a china clay works and loading facility has been incorporated in that tiny scenic area. Yet for all its diminutive size, this 'cameo' layout is not one to feature the small and space-saving pre-Grouping locomotives and stock you might expect. This layout is actually set firmly in

the D&E era with DCC sound-fitted Bo-Bo diesel and single railcars.

Built again to 4mm scale with hand-built EM (18.2mm) trackwork on a cork base, the design harks right back to the thinking behind 'Walke Marine' of a decade earlier, having the visible sceni area fed by multiple track entrances from a pai of fiddle yards arranged at either end of the mai scenic area. Trains on the branch pass from on sector plate to another through the scene. Thos engaged in shunting the sidings of the works are disappear and reappear on scene as the off-scen areas contain the headshunts for the visible sectio as well as representing other parts of the facility. A is powered by one of Bachmann's budget-priced E Command DCC control systems.

The layout, or, more descriptively, 'workin cameo scene', purports to represent part of a branc in the Cheesewring area, in the east of Cornwall. I essence, though, the restricted space of the mode represents little if any of the mystical quality of th true scenic charm of that region. However, enoug of the architectural styles and detail related to typical railway and china clay works have bee incorporated to help set the scene beyond th recognisable rolling stock in use.

The visible area is carefully arranged so that th viewer looks over the front fencing and down th slope into the scene. The scene itself is framed by road overbridge at one end balanced by an area trees at the other (each providing suitable cover fo

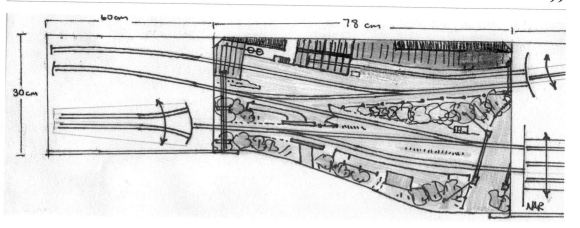

the fiddle yard entrances), and backed by a low-relief representation of several processing and loading buildings of a china clay works. These were created from parts of Metcalf and Walthers kits combined with a degree of scratch-building. The remainder of the structures and details on the model were created from Wills, Hornby, Dapol and Peco components. The scenic vista was created from shaped polystyrene blocks covered in representations of vegetation and

Below: **One of the line's staple traffics, explosives for store, arrives at 'Shell Island'. British Rail motive power is that iconic late-1960s Cambrian loco, the Class 24.** *Neil Rushby*

trees created exclusively from Woodland Scenics products. The vegetation is blended and toned down on the model by light over-sprays of green acrylic paint; likewise all of the trackwork and structures on the model were painted and weathered to suit their particular roles.

The finished scene is illuminated by a fascia shaped to match the layout frontage, and the scenic section and its two associated fiddle yard boards are arranged to sit upon a separate supporting frame with its own folding legs (none of the trio of boards that make up the model are anything like big enough to

have integral folding legs). As with the previously described models, the main scenic board is given a full cover for transport and storage, and the fiddle yard and support structure are designed to break down and bolt together into a minimum of easily handled units for transportation.

Now there is a twist to this model beyond what can be seen in the accompanying photograph. Although shown here featuring an early-1970s pre-TOPS locomotive and rolling stock, the model has actually been designed to support multiple periods. The slowly changing nature of the infrastructure and methods of operation of the prototype branches that inspired this model means that, even with the more modern buildings forming the works, the layout could potentially support any period or rolling stock and operation from around 1960 to the early 1980s, a time span that covers the end of steam in the region right through to the introduction of the Class 37s and high-capacity air-braked hopper wagons. The only physical change needed for the layout to reflect the differing decades would be replacing the road vehicles (primarily the Royal Mail van) with examples appropriate for the time period being portrayed.

Neil's initial plans at the time of writing are to have the early-1970s (pre-TOPS) selection of stock as shown, with weathered and faded green Sulzer Type 2s (drafted in to replace the ailing Class 22s on these lines around 1972), working sheeted china clay opens and a selection of vans of BR and ex-company designs, contrasting with a plain-blue-liveried single unit on the passenger turns. A late-1970s (post-TOPS) set of stock would be very similar, but by then the diesels would be blue, the railcar in post-refurbishment blue and grey, the

china clay wagons modified with sheet rails and new 'hoods', and the vans of all-BR design. For variety one of the last Class 22s could perhaps be added to the stock selection for the early period, and similarly a trip-working 08 shunter for the later. However, if a third period of operation was to be introduced, Nei states that it would likely be best to look back into the 1960s and create a stock selection that would feature the last of steam (be it pannier or 'Prairie' alongside shiny green Class 22s and railcars. I would definitely be a bit of a squeeze, and offer les operational flexibility in the space available with the longer Class 37s and modern air-braked wagons.

The stock prepared so far consists of modified and detailed Bachmann Class 25s, with Hornby o Lima railcars. The sheeted china clay wagons also owe their origins to Bachmann, though the majority of the vans in use are kit-built; all of the stock ha been toned down and weathered with acrylic paint using period photographs as a guide for the finishe required. This helps the stock to blend in with and better suit the overall look of the scene as a whole The latter is an important point, as nothing look worse than completely clean stock in a weathered environment, and vice versa.

The thought behind this model's design was that it would be suitable for the modeller with little or no permanent space for the hobby. The layout could pack away into the smallest of spaces (such as an understairs cupboard or the bottom of a wardrobe) then be quickly erected in a few minutes on a worktop, dining table or similar for operation.

So there you are – proof that prototype-inspired operationally interesting environments in which to run a selection of different trains can be built in even the smallest of areas.

Shell Island
by Neil Rushby

'Shell Island' was built several years ago, and in the intervening period I've written about it both in the model press and on line. So that you don't feel short-changed and I don't bore myself, I thought that I'd look at a couple of features of the layout that haven't had much attention. Given that using small spaces is at the core of this book, I'd like to show how I went about making what is a very small layout look bigger than it is, and describe ways in

which it can maintain 'play value' over and above the seemingly limited scope of two sidings and a cramped kick-back.

'Shell Island' comes in two parts. The scenic section is 2ft 8in long and 1ft 8in deep; the fiddle yard, which we'll come to later, is 2 feet by 1 foot You can see that as a whole the layout is small, bu the scenic section, designed to fit in an alcove at m previous home, is below the size that most would consider viable for an EM-gauge layout. Obviously some compromises have to be made. Trains are short and are comprised of locos and stock that are in themselves also short. I was fortunate that my chosen prototype and era, the Cambrian Coast just after the end of steam, fitted with this requirement – short trains of traditional four-wheeled stock hauled almost exclusively by Class 24 diesels. In such a small space there's not much elbow room for masses of track to sprawl, so I looked at what would be the minimum necessary and resisted the temptation to add to it.

The result was a pair of sidings that diverged from a point close to the edge of the board so that they could be as long as possible. They are also gently angled, which gains a little more space, but this was done to fit in with my vision of how the scene should look rather than for operational reasons. Off the near siding there's a kick-back that serves the goods shed. The headshunt for this is so short that only one of the industrial locos with a single wagon can access the shed. To be honest, this kick-back siding was only included to give a reason to place the goods shed where it is, and the goods shed was required to hide the hole in the backscene where trains leave the layout for the fiddle yard. Making the track plan subservient to the scenery is one of the secrets to making the layout bigger than it is.

You may have noticed from the given dimensions that the layout, though far shorter than normal, is not far off the width of the standard branch-line layout. This relatively generous width helps give a sense of space. Although railway action takes place along almost the entire length of the layout, it only occupies a fraction of the depth, giving room for the scenery to set this action in context. It's no use setting a layout in the Scottish highlands, the East Anglian fens or inner-city London if there's no space to show the location – you might just as well have a train set on the carpet. The real Shell Island is located on the coastal plain of Cardigan Bay, at the mouth of the Afon Artro, set against a backdrop of mountains. Despite putting aside a good proportion of the baseboard area for scenery, there's no room to include but a fraction of this landscape on the layout. This is where a backscene is a must. My model of Shell Island includes the Rhinogs, Cardigan Bay and the mountains of the Lleyn Peninsula, impossible in 3D but eminently achievable in 2D. It's easy to get a sense of great distance in a backscene – the features need to be kept low to the horizon, simple in shape and muted in tone. After painting in the sky, don't bother with clouds, as they will look wrong or distract or both; I pencil in distant hills and paint them with a mix based on the sky blue with a small drop of brown and yellow added. Where the situation warrants I'll sometimes add nearer hills based on the distant hill colour mix with a further drop of yellow. Whether the hills are far away or closer, the sky blue tonal range should be apparent.

I've tried to extend this quest for a spacious look through every aspect of the layout. The basic colouring of the layout is deliberately light in tone – dark shades can look claustrophobic – and the structures are grouped at one end to avoid dominating the scene; again, the colours match the light tones set by the scenery. When it came to adding detail, subservience to the aim of creating a feeling of space and distance was again my priority. There is detail present – at its most basic level it's the variety of textures employed in ground cover. Though there are areas of the layout where nothing is going on, attention to the road surfaces, grass, undergrowth, the water's edge and the water itself ensures that the basics aren't bland. The more conventional detail, the small objects placed about the layout to suggest life, have all been selected to be undemonstrative. There are boats, one quietly moored on the mud bank, one part way through repainting, and a couple of pots of paint suggest that a tea break may be in progress. A couple chat outside the café, watched by a cat. Drinks crates are stacked by the door, waiting to be dealt with. The goods shed is free from obvious signs of trade and commerce, but the door is slid open a fraction, giving a glimpse into the cool shadows inside. Busy details that clamour for attention would swamp a small layout; by keeping them subtle and understated they add life but don't destroy the illusion of space.

Operation could seem a bit pointless; after all, there's not much space for the trains to stretch their legs. A shuttle between the off-scene fiddle yard and the end of the sidings gives a run of just over 4 feet less the length of the train. The basic premise is that traffic is exchanged between British Rail and RAE Llanbedr, which receives stores by rail. The traffic is mainly coal for fuel and explosives, which the RAE is contracted to store to even out variation in demand. Explosives travel in vans so there's little I can do to show what's going on. Coal, however, is a different matter, and it's simple to provide removable loads so that the ebb and flow of fulls and empties can be depicted. It's surprised me just how much more fun and purpose has been injected into the layout by this simple addition. Like the discipline exercised in keeping the look of the layout pared down and spacious, I've also kept the traffic and stock limited. Indulging in all sorts of fancies would destroy any illusion of reality that I might have captured.

'Below: **St Minions'** is a very effective little layout specifically designed for the modeller with little or no permanent space for the hobby. *Steve Flint, courtesy of Railway Modeller*

Above: **Having collected the full wagons, the shunter returns a couple of empties. While this activity is taking place, the BR loco crew have a welcome break.** *Neil Rushby*

The Gwynedd Railway
A mid-1970s 4mm Welsh narrow-gauge layout
by Malcolm Clarke

In the mid-1970s, having built an exhibition layout with my school model railway society and having recently bought a small modern house, I decided to embark on a small exhibition layout. It was to be a first attempt at a complete layout containing a mixture of old and new ideas chosen for their ability to portray the Welsh narrow gauge. Although the layout did not represent any particular line, it did at least embody most of the features so typical of the turn-of-the-century narrow-gauge scene.

When the layout was first started, the scale was fixed by the availability of commercial narrow gauge items running on 9mm track. The basic requirements borne in mind during construction were:

- it must be easily portable, giving ease of assembly for exhibition purposes.
- it must have small baseboards – maximum size 36 by 20 inches – for manoeuvrability within the confines of a modern house, and a maximum layout length of 13ft 6in.
- the baseboards must be transported in a stack rather than a crate so that the layout could be stored in the small third bedroom; the stack was used as a layout support.
- baseboards to be accurately aligned using steel dowels similar to pattern-makers dowels.
- a rigid sub-base for the trackwork.
- reliable operation to dispel the theory that narrow-gauge layouts never run well.
- a self-contained lighting system using fluorescent tubes.
- the visible portion to comprise sweeping curves so typical of the narrow gauge; tight curves were needed at each end of the layout but these were in tunnels.
- trains would run round from the fiddle yard, crossing in the loop, then continue back to the fiddle yard. This enabled locos to run in one direction only as it was found that most locos run better in one direction than the other. Shunting was to be kept to a minimum.
- the fiddle yard was to comprise two roads, one for each direction of running, with three trains stored in each; trains were shuttled along the roads by the operator.

Baseboard construction followed well-tried methods of using 2-by-1-inch framing with a top surface of half-inch chipboard. The chipboard was only cut away where the scenery fell below baseboard level, ensuring maximum rigidity. To ensure realism, care was taken to plan the scenery detail before the boards were built. The framework was glued together with Resin W woodworking glue, which was used for almost every job on the layout, and clamped with sash clamps until the glue set. The chipboard was then glued and screwed down to the framework. The baseboard dimensions were set at 36 by 20 inches, smaller than usual, but with care taken in alignment of the end profiles of the boards no problem was encountered with gaping joints.

The ends of the boards were fitted with plywood profiles clamped together in pairs for adjoining boards and cut to the contour desired for the scenery.

The method of assembly was to glue and pin one scenery profile to one baseboard, making sure that the plywood mated up with the ends of the board and that the track bases lined up. When the adhesive was cured, the second baseboard was carefully removed and its dowel plate bolted on. The second scenery profile was coated with Resin W and placed in position. The boards were then clamped together and the profiles adjusted to mate up before being left to dry. Before the clamps were removed, two quarter-inch holes were drilled to take the securing bolts used to clamp the boards together.

Tracklaying was undertaken next, and this followed the usual methods. The layout was drawn full size onto paper, then transferred to the chipboard trackbase. Cork was not used, as a solid base was preferred. Copper-clad sleeper strip was cut to length and laid down along the track centre-line, alignment being checked by eye. PVA adhesive was used for this. The position of tie bars for points was marked on the boards and slots were cut through the track base to accommodate the rocking lever used to operate the points. Flat-bottomed rail (Code 65 BH N/S is best) was soldered down. The points were built with the common crossings laid first, and the wing and closure rails being set up from the crossings. Finally the stock rails and switch blades were set up.

The track was wired on the cab control system using two controllers, and was thoroughly tested and adjusted. Once satisfactory performance was obtained, the track was painted and ballasted. The trackwork was thoroughly cleaned of all flux deposits and painted with track colour on the sleepers and rust on the rail sides. The rail tops were cleaned before the paint could dry. N-scale granite chippings were used for ballast, mixed with Polycell wallpaper paste and applied with a screwdriver. This took a long time, but the results were worthwhile. The track proved to be reliable and reasonable running was achieved.

Above: Scenery at its very best! The whole scene looks so real – the cottages, the track, the slate wall and, of course, the train itself. *Malcolm Clarke*

Right: Again, note the superb scenery. Especially look at the slate fencing which is so typical of the prototype scene on such railways as the Talyllyn. *Malcolm Clarke*

Below: Plan of 'The Gwynedd Railway'. 1 Road, 2 Level crossing, 3 Goods shed, 4 Station building, 5 Water tower, 6 Stables, 7 Canal, 8 Road, 9 Farm, 10 River, 11 Control

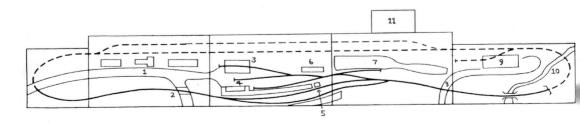

The basic scenery was started next. A general outline had been decided on before layout construction commenced. Edge profiles for the sides of the boards were prepared and fitted in place, and the outline of the scenery formed in polystyrene blocks.

Once the polystyrene blocks had been cut to shape and secured to the layout, they were covered with strips of plasterer's scrim, which was glued to the scenery profiles with Evostik impact adhesive. A thin layer of hardwall plaster was spread over the surface. When this had dried out, a 50% solution of Resin W was made up and applied to seal the surface of the plaster. An 80% PVA/20% water coating was then added to the areas to be grassed, and sifted sawdust that had been dyed green was sprinkled on; two coats were required. Loose material was vacuumed up and used again. Various shades of Woodland Scenics scatter materials were then used. For soil or paths carefully sifted potting compost was mixed with Resin W and applied with a knife. Use was made of mosses and lichens, which were preserved in a 50% solution of glycerol, to represent various ferns and grasses.

The water effects were achieved by using both varnish (for the streams) and casting resin (for the canal). In the latter case a large, flat expanse was required. The shape of the canal was cut out of the baseboard and hardboard glued to the underside to form the bottom. The side walls were formed of scribed hardwall plaster and the bottom and towpath were made of the same material. After painting the bottom murky brown, the bed was sealed with a coating of Resin W. The water was then formed of two or three layers of clear casting resin. Weeds and various objects were incorporated in each layer to give the effect of depth.

Drystone walls were constructed from broken pieces of shale extracted in lumps from the Pennines. Resin W was used as the adhesive. This shale is very effective as its colouring is a good representation of slate. Rock outcrops were formed by using pieces of real stone – you can't beat the real thing!

The buildings were constructed from hardwall plaster cast into slabs for each wall, then scribed with a pin before being glued together. Roofing slates were individual pieces of grey paper.

The locomotive stock was based upon proprietary examples available at the time, and with either 0-4-0 or 0-6-0 wheel arrangements so that they could negotiate the 8-inch-radius curves in the tunnels at each end of the layout. During the many exhibitions attended these curves gave no trouble at all.

The most reliable chassis proved to be Arnold and Fleischmann. With one or two exceptions, the locomotives were assembled from white metal kits.

The coaching stock was mainly assembled from modified Ratio GWR four-wheeled coaches suitably cut down and fitted with interiors. There is now a large number of excellent kits available and the 9mm gauge modeller is well supported by the '009' Society.

Many of the techniques used in the layout were developed from ideas suggested by other people and, in particular, fellow members of Rochdale Model Railway Group. Looking back I often regret that I succumbed to building larger layouts, as Gwynedd proved popular on the exhibition circuit; it was easy to transport and maintain and, most importantly, ran reliably.

Bilston Road Engine Shed
by Peter Cullen

Like many modellers I have always owned more locomotives than are required to operate my layout, a situation that can only be exacerbated by the very high quality of models now being offered by our leading manufacturers. Back in 1990, when this engine shed layout was built, my main layout was a non-portable end-to-end one that fitted snugly into the third bedroom, or Railway Room

as it has always been known. The locomotives that were not in use on the layout were stored in boxes underneath, an unsatisfactory state of affairs as storing and removing locos from boxes on a regular basis can and did lead to unnecessary damage and the wasting of valuable modelling time.

Some serious thought was given to the best way to resolve this issue and the chance discovery of two pieces of 6 feet by 1 foot mahogany-coated chipboard in a skip indicated a way forward. They were promptly commandeered, and while one board was stored in the loft for possible future use I set about building an engine shed on the other. I had no plans for this layout to be exhibited and had in fact never considered that anyone may be interested in looking at anything I had built. When finished I planned that the layout would sit on a shelf in the Railway Room and be little more than a diorama, although I decided that an interesting project would be to provide many dead sections so that the layout could be operated if required; this was of course long before DCC .

Peco track and points were laid to make maximum use of the limited space, with a fiddle yard of just one siding. Points were operated by wire-in-tube, with the wire ends poking through the baseboard edge. The space between the tracks was built up using balsa wood and a thick coating of ground cover material. A small track diagram was stencilled onto the outside of the rear backscene with 16 simple on/off switches inserted into the diagram to control the various sections. The main engine shed was built from four ancient Airfix (now Dapol) kits, while the coaling stage was a further side section of the Airfix kit modified and with a tank added to the roof. The whole scene was surrounded by a small brick wall with Peco city backscenes adding depth. When complete, the layout sat on the shelf in the Railway Room at eye level providing the storage and display facility that I required, and remained undisturbed apart from an occasional dusting for the next 14 years.

Fast forward now to 2004. My 'Skip Hill' layout, which had been built on the other board, was established on the exhibition circuit and I was asked if I had another small layout that was both easy and cheap to transport. I realised that as the engine shed could use the trestles, lighting

Plan of 'Bilton Road Engine Shed'. 1 Engine shed, 2 Coaling stage, 3 Control panel

and drapes of 'Skip Hill', it should be possible bring the layout to a reasonable standard witho too much difficulty and would be a way of showir off my locomotives, which are all ready-to-ru but have all been heavily weathered by Sutto Coldfield Railway Society member Martin Smit The layout was livened up by the addition of a impressive name board, which proudly proclaim

BRITISH RAILWAYS (WESTERN REGION BILSTON ROAD ENGINE SHED

and further details were added to the layout itse including a colour light signal to control acce to the fiddle yard and some dummy point leve together with a few figures including a photograph standing on a pallet looking over the wall.

Operation of the layout is surprising interesting, with locomotives coming off the fidd yard and queuing up for the coaling stage. Aft coaling, the loco is moved onto the ashpit, then the shed. In the meantime another locomotive sent off shed and into the fiddle yard to be eith removed from the track or to reappear later. It quite possible to jam up the shed totally, somethir I am sure must have happened in steam days.

I have to confess that I am not a great lov of the engine shed type of layout – I prefer a litt more action, ideally with a small tank engi banging a few wagons round a yard (although th must have a purpose). However, I am convinc that an engine shed is a suitable first project is ideal as a change of pace for when progress o the great master plan has stalled; if the modeller short of space or enjoys locomotive constructio then this is an obvious solution. By the autumn 2009 the brief exhibition career of 'Bilston Ro Engine Shed' appeared to be over after around te appearances, and it returned to its previous state inactivity. It was fun while it lasted and bizarr is still the only layout I have built that someo wanted to buy from me.

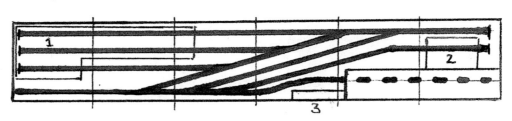

An overall view of 'Bilston Road Engine Shed'. *Andy Smyth*

A close-up view of pannier tank No 4672 on shed. Note the detail, which is so important on a small layout. *Andy Smyth*

Skip Hill Mineral Railway
by Peter Cullen

This little railway was inspired by the Cromford & High Peak line in Derbyshire. I have long been interested in the line and have visited the site to walk and bike-ride the High Peak Trail on several occasions, in particular the fearsome 1 in 14 gradient of Hopton incline, which has been well documented in books, DVDs and videos, and cried out to be modelled. For several years I had sketched plans on the backs of envelopes, beer mats and other assorted pieces of waste paper. I particularly wanted to build this layout on a single board that would be reasonably easy to transport should it ever get finished and should I be fortunate enough to be asked to show it at an exhibition. A quick search of the loft unearthed the second 6 feet by 1 foot piece of chipboard (see 'Bilston Road Engine Shed' above) that had been liberated from the skip in 1990, and the appearance and slow running qualities of the Hornby 'J94', a class of locomotive that was used extensively on the Cromford & High Peak, convinced me that the time for planning and doodling was over and it was time to get something built.

The first requirement was to ascertain whether the loco would pull three mineral wagons up a 1 in 14 gradient. Fortunately the answer was yes, and I soon had the track laid using Peco code

75. The track layout is basically an elongated 'Z' with head shunts and sidings just long enough to accommodate a 'J94' loco and three mineral wagons, and with a two-siding fiddle yard under the high level at the rear of the layout. The high level has three sidings, one of which is under a corrugated-iron shed arrangement that allows the empty wagons to be loaded out of view of an observer. Similarly, in the fiddle yard the wagons can be unloaded out of sight so the observer will see short trains of empty mineral wagons being propelled to the high level while full mineral wagons are taken back down the steep gradient supposedly to some exchange sidings but in reality to the hidden fiddle yard. As I was particularly keen for operation on the layout to be as hands free as possible, the locos and wagons were all fitted with MSE automatic couplings; however as the wagons all run in rakes of three, three-link couplings are used within the rakes with the MSE couplings only on the outer ends. After some initial teething problems caused by my inability to read the instructions before fitting the couplings, they have proved to be totally successful.

The layout also features a canal wharf and siding on the lower level, and shunting the wharf siding makes an interesting diversion from attacking the gradients. The wharf siding is usually shunted by a Gem/Branchlines North London tank locomotive constructed by Sutton Coldfield Railway society member Ted Hastilow. This class of locomotive was also in regular use on the line. The goods shed on the canal wharf which has a fully detailed and illuminated interior bears a more than passing resemblance to the shed at Cromford. The headshunt at the top end of the first gradient features a scratch-built workshop with a detailed and illuminated interior together with a couple of small Wills buildings and a couple

Plan of 'Skip Hill Mineral Railway'. 1 Goods shed (low level), 2 Canal wharf, 3 Exit to fiddle yard under high-level lines, 4 Workshops (middle level), 5 Gravel loader (high level), 6 Gravel loader/control panel

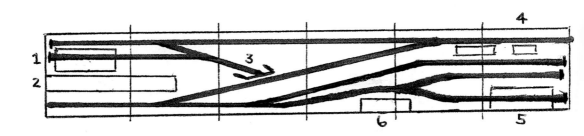

lovely view of one of the small locos used at **Skip Hill**.
ndy Smyth

f derelict and grounded narrow-gauge wagons.
he top level features the gravel loaders and a
ouple of small platforms where a spot of welding
taking place. A DJH Andrew Barclay is usually
nployed in sorting out the empty and full wagons
hile the 'J94' takes on water. A Connoisseur Kits
implex petrol loco, also built by Ted Hastilow, sits
t the end of the long siding with an open wagon
ontaining ballast and track tools and makes an
ccasional sortie up to the headshunt where some
ack maintenance is being undertaken.

All points on this layout are electrically
perated via mini toggle switches on a track
iagram on the rear of the backscene. There are
umerous dead sections, so almost full cab control
as been achieved. The long planning paid off and
have only had to make one very minor alteration
 the wiring, which was more of a 'that would be
ice' than a 'desperately needed'. One feature of
his layout that I greatly enjoy is the sound system.

This is an Express Models product sadly no longer
in production due to the unavailability of one of
the components. It was a little fiddly to install on
the finished layout and would have been easier
fitted at the tracklaying stage rather than when
the scenery was finished. However, the result has
been more than worth the effort involved, with
volume control and length of beat adjustable, and
a beat that increases as more current is drawn and
the locomotive speed increases. There is also a
satisfying hiss when the locomotive is stationary.
The sound system has added a whole new
dimension to operating the layout.

I have been fortunate enough to have exhibited
this layout more than 30 times. With my co-
operators from Sutton Coldfield Railway Society
we usually work 1 hour on, 1 hour off. The hour
of operating can be absorbing and always seems to
pass quickly. For a train of empty wagons to exit the
fiddle yard, ascend to the summit, be shunted, and
for the locomotive to collect the full wagons and
descend back to the fiddle yard can easily take 20
minutes as all movements are carried out as slowly as

An 'Austerity' 0-6-0 climbs the bank to the higher level. I think it is these banks that make this layout so fascinating. Pete has been very ingenious in packing a lot into a small space. *Andy Smyth*

possible. In total the train has covered almost 50 feet – not bad for a 6-foot layout! I am often asked what I have done to achieve such slow running, and the answer is to clean the wheels scrupulously and clean the track, with regular maintenance and lubrication of the locomotive (ensuring that no lubricant finds its way to the track, for obvious reasons).

'Skip Hill' has given me a great deal of enjoyment over the years. There is much to be said in favour of building a small layout that will

be finished in a reasonable time span, is quick an easy to assemble, and is also interesting to operate While I have nothing but admiration for thos dedicated modellers who spend years producin one great masterpiece, I am more than happy wit my modest achievement. After all the doodling the finished layout has exceeded my expectations

Port Foxdale
OOn3 scale (4mm to the foot on 12mm gauge track)
by Robin G. Winter

Size matters, and for a number of years building small layouts had no appeal whatsoever; indeed, when in the past I modelled standard gauge, as most of us start, size certainly mattered. That is until we moved to our present home, when my dear wife posted 'part two orders' and I was presented with a bookcase top, 5ft 3in long by 12 inches deep. That was where the new model layout was to be built!

It is true to say that all I wanted was somethin on which to run my favourite Manx locomotive: but to build a representation of the Isle of Ma Railway, for which I had more than 40 year of interest, enthusiasm, obsession and love was possibly stretching the point on this size o baseboard… I had then to take the option that m very unique prototype railway was going to have t fit this bookcase top or not at all, and that was not an ongoing option!

I had never really been restricted for space with any model railway, and to be honest at first I had this notion that fitting my ideas on a narrow-gauge railway into a small space would be easy. How wrong I was!

I soon realised, however, that despite lack of real running space compared with, for instance, a 'club layout' track, I was going to be able to consider a good amount of scenic space, so much so that I found a place to build a picture-postcard view of the Manx landscape to fit 'around' my railway. Something I hold valuable with any layout of any size I build, the scenery has to complement the railway, not a railway without scenery or its environment.

The minimum space layout can still provide enough space to build true like-for-like as far as a prototype is concerned. However, what I had to consider was that, with the inclusion of a fiddle yard, a baseboard of this size was never ever going to provide a prototype run-round loop. Consider then the 14-coach trains with a locomotive or two, as was the case on the prototype. The compromise had to be made and it was decided to build a scenically prototypical Manx look-alike layout, but a fictitious terminus. By this time, with the inclusion of a fiddle yard, I had but 4 feet to build the Isle of Man!

Having scoured books and my photographs taken over several decades, the line at Port Foxdale was conceived. This fictitious line was to take the shape of a northern terminus of a proposed secondary route that runs around the back of St John's. It enters the harbour at Port Foxdale (Glen Wyllin in reality) below the Manx Northern Railway Viaduct, which was a prototypical piece of engineering some 60 feet above ground level.

The quay was inspired by the inner harbour wall at Port St Mary, and was built to transfer products from the Foxdale group of lead, zinc and silver mines to take the pressure off Ramsey. The harbour light is from Port Erin, at the south of the island.

I did concede to the use of the two prototype buildings on the true Foxdale branch. The station building and water tower both sat at the idyllic Foxdale village, and the station building still does, as it serves as a Community Centre.

There is nothing extraordinary about the scenery construction compared with other modellers. I used Peco HOm track; a disadvantage was that the turnouts should really have been of the 'Y' format, but that is a minor detail. The permanent way is comprised of rail-level ground covering or grass.

The beach and sea bed I have to admit once adorned Douglas beach! I had this real desire to make it as scenically correct as possible, but did I get some questions at Ronaldsway Airport!

I often get asked where the boat comes from; well, it cost just £1.50 at one of those seaside souvenir shops. The hull is wood and a superb 'small trawler' shape. The top was discarded, the sides dug out to give a thinner side, and styrene replacement fittings were added.

The layout is set during the fragile 1960s and '70s when real threats of closure loomed over the whole system. In 1965 closure did come, with both rolling stock and infrastructure in a dreadful state. Fortunately this closure was to be short-lived as in 1967 the railway reopened with locomotives out-shopped in an Apple Green not too dissimilar from the LNER livery. This has given great scope for alternating the operation of the layout at exhibitions, using the 1945 Indian Red so prominent from my youth, and the later 'Ailsa' Green, of which I have very fond memories from my teens.

One of the delights of building a model of the Isle of Man Railway, certainly up to circa 1978, is the very real backwards glance at road vehicles and road signs. Still in everyday use were Commer vans, Thornycroft lorries, Ford Anglias and Utility buses out of the Ark. All make for some very pleasant out-of-the-ordinary model-making.

At its peak the Isle of Man Railway had some 47 route miles of 3-foot-gauge railway, and 15 very beautifully and typically crafted Beyer Peacock 2-4-0 locomotives. In addition there is one Dubs & Co 0-6-0 tank, used very little but a significant member of the locomotive fleet. In addition there are 75 bogie coaches from various sources, and numerous goods vehicles, some having been built in-house at Douglas.

For the most part the initial model rolling stock that was required to run Port Foxdale was built prior to any scenery, really to satisfy myself that I could replicate my obsession in 4mm

Above: **An overall view of 'Port Foxdale' which shows what a marvellous small layout it is.** *Robin Winter*

Below: **Plan of 'Port Foxdale'. Note the scenic break provided by Glen Wyllin Viaduct carrying the Douglas-Ramsey line northwards (towards the rear of the layout). The layout is operated from the front left-hand side.**

to the foot and have successful running. I had certain prototypes that were a must – those that I had driven or otherwise. When I started this project, only George E. Mellor was producing kits suitable for the Isle of Man Railway, and these were becoming hard to find. However, by the 1990s other enthusiastic Manx modellers gave manufacturers enough of a push to allow for all 16 locomotives to be available in white metal and brass kit form from Branchlines, and almost all the variants of coaches from Roxey Mouldings in brass etched kit form. The locomotive kits all needed much 'rearrangement' to suit rebuilds and 'parts' exchange as seen on the prototype locomotives

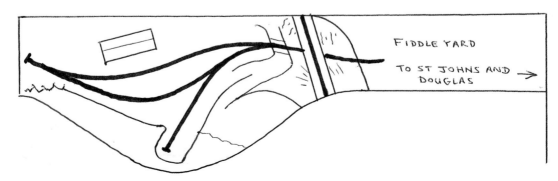

FIDDLE YARD

TO ST JOHNS AND DOUGLAS →

This left some gaps, but I guess most of us enjoy some kind of scratch-building on our layouts, and with this layout the task was extremely enjoyable.

I have probably gone over the top with rolling stock for such a small layout, mainly on the grounds that my interest just kept rolling. I have built all 16 of the locomotives, a far cry from the five I promised myself I would build to suit those very fond memories from the early 1970s, especially the driving of No 10 G. H. Wood in 1974.

Locomotives that might also have been explored, and those like No 17 *Viking*, the Schoema diesel that arrived in the 1990s, have been built. The body was etched for me by Worsley Works and the rest of the loco scratch-built.

Also scratch-built from Ireland was a 'might have been' in addition to the two County Donegal railcars. The West Clare Railway had closed and had three diesels for sale; well, it never happened for the IMR, except on 'Port Foxdale'.

Some goods vehicles are available, but the rest are down to

Above: **No 6 Peverill** in the station. Look at the wealth of detail in the photograph. *Robin Winter*

Below: **No 8 Fenella** in front of the station. *Robin Winter*

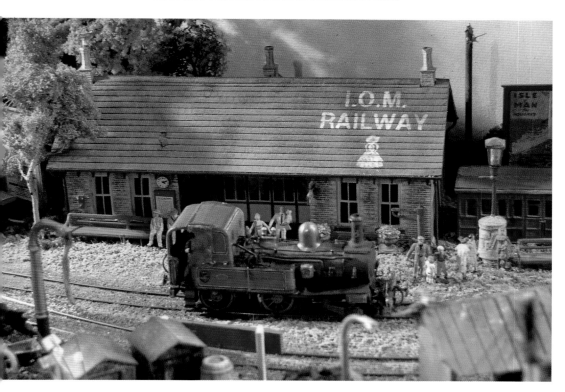

the modeller, with a vast amount of superb scratch-building opportunities.

So, would I build another small-space layout? The answer is most certainly yes – in fact, I have done just that with a more recent layout. It is just a case of thinking big in a small space.

My wife and I have exhibited 'Port Foxdale' for almost 10 years and in that time have been lucky enough to win a number of trophies. This has been a real bonus to the interest from the viewing public. We were winners of the Reinier Herndricksen Trophy at ExpoNG in 2001, 'Most Exotic Layout' at Expometrique in Paris in 2003, and Best Layout at Amberley in 2004/5. It has also appeared in a number of model railway magazines around Europe.

For those interested in modelling the Isle of Man Railway, the following may be of use.

Boyd, J. I. C. **The Isle of Man Railway** (Centenary Edition) (Oakwood Press, 1973, no ISBN)
    The Isle of Man Railway Volumes 1 (0 85361 444 X), 2 (0 85361 469 5) and 3 (0 85361 479 2) (Oakwood Press, 1993, 1994 and 1996 respectively)
    On the Isle of Man Narrow Gauge (Bradford Barton, 1978; 0 85153 363 9)
Hendry, Robert **Rails in the Isle of Man** (Midland Publishing, 1993; 1 85780 009 5)
    British Railway Signalling (Midland Publishing, 2001; 1 85780 114 8)
Hendry, R. Preston and R. Powell **Isle of Man Railway Album** (David & Charles, 1976; 0 7153 682281)
    Manx Northern Railway (Hillside Publishing, 1980; 9505933 2 X)
Hill, R. L. and Patrick, D. **Beyer, Peacock – Locomotive Builders to the World** (Transport Publishing Co, 1982; 0 903839 41 5)
Isle of Man Tourist Brochure (IoM Tourist Board, annually)
Lloyd-Jones, David **The Manx Peacocks** (Atlantic, 1998; 0 906899 95 8)
    Introduction to Modelling the Isle of Man Railway (Warners/BRM, 1996; 0 9514144 3 7)
McNab, Ian **History of the Isle of Man Railway** (Green Lake Publications, 1945; no ISBN)
Winter, Robin G. **Isle of Man Railway: A Modeller's Inspiration** (Peco Publications, 2008; ISBN 9780900586958)
Ward Lock & Co Ltd **The Isle of Man Red Guide**

Railway Modeller (Peco Publications)
January 1988: County Donegal railcars Nos 19 and 20 (scale drawings by Ian Beattie)
May 1993: IoMR 2-4-0T No 1 *Sutherland* (scale drawings by Ian Beattie)
May 1995: IoMR 0-6-0T No 15 *Caledonia* (scale drawings by Ian Beattie)
March 2004: Part 1 'The Isle of Man Railway – a modeller's inspiration'
June 2004: Part 2 'The permanent way'
June 2004: The E vans (with scale drawings by Jonathan Joseph)
January 2005: Part 3 'Signalling'
January 2006: Part 4 'The diesel railcars Nos 19 and 20'
July 2006: 'Santon station' – suggested layout (Plan of the month)
October/November/December 2006: 'Ramsey' (OOn3 layout) by Alan Catlow (parts 1-3)
November 2006: Part 6 'No 17 *Viking* – a German immigrant (with scale drawings by Andrew Beard)
October 2007: Part 7 'Moving the modelling forward – additions to the layout and stock' (This occasional series continues)

Bottrill Street Yard
by Nigel Adams

I have built two previous layouts of this name, but they were in O gauge, while this one was in Gn15 scale. The name is the same because the layout used the professionally made nameboard from the O gauge layouts, which was simply too good to sit in the shed gathering dust!

I have always been attracted to layouts in Gn15 scale probably because, for many years, I modelled in 0-16.5. Also the small size of a Gn15 layout means that it is easily transported to shows with all the necessary stock, toolboxes, etc, in a family-size car together with my fellow operator.

I also felt that a small Gn15 layout would be a welcome change from my usual O-gauge layouts. The die was cast when a friend told me he was selling his Gn15 loco and rolling stock. I bought it at a very reasonable price, so had to build a layout! It had to be one that was easily stored in my shed and transportable to exhibitions.

The idea for the layout came from a book about Sir Arthur Henderson's railway in the early 20th century. The track plan was very simple and portrayed a 15-inch-gauge line running from the squire's house through the grounds down to the road to make it easier to bring up supplies. There was a passing loop, an unloading platform and two sidings, one of which was used for servicing the locos. The unloading platform was in a yard near the road and the squire's grandson (Jesse) has his grandfather's permission to establish a business there restoring and selling Morris Minor cars and vans.

Once again, I went about designing the layout in the wrong way! I had an existing board from a previous layout measuring 38 by 22 inches, so I designed the layout to fit this, saving time and money. As can be seen from the plan, the track ran diagonally across the board from top right to bottom left. The cassette areas were hinged to each end of the main board for storage and transport. When erected, the layout measured 66 by 22 inches and was operated from the rear.

The four cassettes were made from plywood. Each cassette was powered by a wander lead, one end of which plugged into a socket at each end of the main board, while at the other end there were two crocodile clips that clipped onto two bolts on the cassette side facing outwards; these bolts were in turn wired to the track on the cassette. I found this simple but effective. The ends of the cassettes were shaped to fit into the opening in the end backscene boards to locate them, and this worked well. The backscene was made from plywood strengthened by 15mm square timber along the top. This not only strengthened the backscene timber, but provided somewhere for me to clip on the lights I used at exhibitions.

The board was supported on two 'H' legs made from 2-by-1-inch timber. These were bolted to the main board and movement was avoided by holding them in place with two diagonal braces (also 2 by 1 inches) and a plywood shelf that fitted underneath the main board and rested on the horizontal leg braces. Each cassette board was held in place by a piece of 2-by-1-inch timber cantilevered off the bottom horizontal crosspiece on each leg. The cantilever timber was joined to the leg and the cassette by a hinge at the top and bottom with removable pins. Further strength was added by a piece of plywood bolted to the front of the cassette area and the front of the main board.

For storage and transport a framed plywood 'lid' was bolted onto the 15mm square timber of

Plan of 'Bottrill Street Yard'. 1 Stone walls, 2 Low-relief buildings, 3 Unloading platform, 4 Building, 5 Wooden fence, 6 Sales area of refurbished Morris Minors, 7 To cassettes

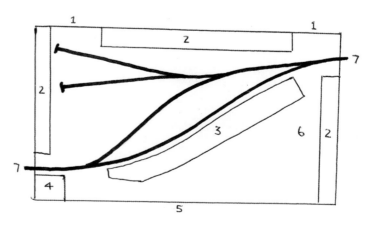

Above: **A view of 'Bottrill Street Yard' looking towards the left-hand cassette area. The exit is hidden from view by the buildin on the left, and the unloading platform and the loco roads are also visible.** *Author*

the backscene. This also allowed me to put plastic boxes on the 'lid' when taking the layout to an exhibition, thus saving room in the car.

The track was all Peco 0-16.5 and the points were hand-operated using welding rod. Initially I relied on blade contact for electrical continuity – a big mistake. I should have known better! Fortunately two friends came to my aid and modified the point wiring and fitted slide switches. The welding rod fitted into a small hole drilled in the slider on the switch. Problem solved! The control panel was built onto the rear of the main boarding at the wider part of the triangular area that resulted from the track layout. There was room here too for the DIN plug for the 'walkabout' controller to plug into, and four sockets – two for the main power into the layout and two for the wheel-cleaning brush. There was also a small plastic box glued to the baseboard in which to keep small things such as the lunch tickets, etc, at shows.

The track was ballasted with Woodland Scenic ballast in the usual way – laid loose and held dow with a mixture of white glue, water and a littl washing-up liquid applied with an eye-droppe When set hard the surplus was removed with small screwdriver and vacuumed up.

On such a small layout the electrical side wa very simple – there were just two feeds and fou dead sections.

The buildings, such as they were, were all low relief and made from foamboard used for advertisin placards, which is very light and strong. It wa covered with proprietary plastic sheet representin stonework or corrugated sheet painted to suit.

The backscene was from International Mode and was very effective. The platform was mad from balsa wood and faced with plastic stone sheet The fence along the front of the layout was mad from plastic sheet and the advertising hoarding were made by cutting down a large advertisin postcard produced by Arriva Trains (Wales) Ltd, which featured old posters used by the Great Western Railway to advertise the Welsh resorts that it served. The surface of the area between the platform and the fence was made from plastic paved sheet and looked effective when 'dirtied up'.

As always on my layouts, I like adding scenic detail and I obtained most of the items I used (as well as most of the rolling stock) from 'Back 2 Bay 6' in Telford. The rest I bought at shows.

The Morris Minors sold by the squire's grandson were bought from various places and I used my labelling machine to make up small 'price tags' for each vehicle on display.

With the exception of two Hornby locos (*Bill and Ben*), which I converted into open-cab locos, all the locos and rolling stock were kits from Back 2 Bay 6'. Each of the locos was powered by a Tenshodo 'Spud' chassis, which was simply fixed to the underside of the body with 'Blu-Tack'! I also

bought a Bachmann 0n30 loco, for which 'Back 2 Bay 6' produces a conversion body kit. That too worked out well.

The beauty of this layout was that all the stock could be carried in a small plastic toolbox! This, together with the usual things you take to exhibitions, such as lighting, tools, spare controllers, transformers, etc, easily fitted in my car together with the overnight bags for me and my fellow operator. The layout was also light and did not take long to set up and dismantle, which was a big bonus.

Sadly the layout is no more! I decided to change it to a 'round-and-round' one and added hidden sidings at the back. It appeared at three shows in this guise, but for some reason I was never quite happy with it. Then my wife said, 'You know, this isn't one of the best layouts you've built!' This confirmed a feeling that had been on my mind for some time, so I dismantled it and started to build a new one on a 4-by-2-foot baseboard.

Below: **A view looking towards the refurbished Morris Minor cars for sale. I have found that features such as this become a talking point at shows with comments like 'We had one of those' or 'Grandad used to have a car like that'.** *Author*

The Shed
An O-gauge layout on an ironing board
by Nigel Adams

In the mid-1960s I built an 009 layout on an ironing board (see pages 60-62 of *Layouts for Limited Spaces*) and it seemed to generate quite a bit of interest at exhibitions. In the late 1990s I built another layout on an ironing board ('Bottrill Street Yard Mark 2'). Therefore it is probably no surprise that, when I was passing our local 'end of line shop' and noticed an ironing board, I bought it for £6. The original idea was to build a Gn15 layout, but then madness set in and I thought of building a simple O-gauge layout on it! It is now one of my current exhibition layouts.

It is perhaps an overstatement to call it a layout – perhaps a better description might be a 'working diorama'. Whatever you call it, it is simply two lengths of Peco track with a cassette area at each end, and depicts part of a loco shed. The cassette areas are hidden by plywood painted black on which I can display notices and the 'Can you find…?' list of items.

The backscene boards are made of plywood and strengthened by 15mm square timber at the top, which also allows me to clip on two spotlights at shows.

The layout was very simple and quick to construct and the buildings were made from Heljan engine shed parts that I had in my store cupboard, either new or from previous layouts I had dismantled.

The 'electrics' are very simple. Each track has a feed and a number of dead sections on it. The switches are set in a length of aluminium angle screwed to the back of the backscene. I have used this method of fixing switches before and find it very simple and effective.

The 'ballast' is Polyfilla mixed with black poster paint and applied with an old knife and my finger!

As this is such a small layout I believe it is necessary to have plenty of scenic detail to hold people's attention – in any case, I like adding scenic detail. An Airfix water tower hides the entrance from the left-hand side as you look at it from the front, and an old tanker body is used as an overhead water tank on one of the shed buildings on the right. There are lights in two of the low relief buildings and an arc-welder and a flashing light in two other buildings. There is a 'Can you find…?' list for those who like that sort of thing – and I find that there is an increasing number of people at shows who do. (The list for this layout is reproduced on page 68.)

Right: **A view looking down on 'The Shed'. The roof at the bottom right of the photo is that of another shed (made from Heljan 'bits'), which hides the exit to the cassette area at that end of the layout.** *Author*

Opposite page: **A view showing how a 'bricked-up' window can be different and effective. Note also the tank on top of the roof.** *Author*

Believe it or not, the layout is operated to a very simple sequence timetable and, personally, I find it quite relaxing to sit behind the layout 'shuffling locos around'!

As with 'Bottrill Street Yard', one of the reasons it is called 'The Shed' is that I had a previous layout of that name and still had the professionally made nameboard, and it seemed a shame to waste it.

The only change I have made since building the layout is that it is no longer supported on the ironing board legs. I already had a support frame measuring 45 by 22 inches that I use for other layouts, and which was the support frame for the original 'The Shed' layout. This is much more sturdy than the ironing board's folding legs, and as the ironing board was only 12 inches wide, this has allowed me to add a 10-inch-wide shelf at the rear of the layout on which to store locos, small tools, etc, and the occasional drink!

However, the ironing board legs are not wasted. I had a piece of Contiboard in the shed which was just the right length and width to replace the ironing board top. I screwed this to the legs and now have a small stock table to take to shows.

At the same time I also extended the layout slightly using a piece of Contiboard. I had some

scenic items in store and it seemed an ideal opportunity to use them. There is no track on this board, which measures 31 by 9 inches, and it is bracketed off the front of the original board and supported at the front by a piece of broomstick. It gives the layout additional depth as viewers have to 'look through' the scenic items on the board to see the locos moving. I also took the opportunity to place six road vehicles there to give added interest. For the younger generation one of the figures on the extension board is the Fat Controller!

'The Shed' made its exhibition debut at the West Wales exhibition in August 2008. It is so easy to transport, carry and set up, and as you get older a layout such as this becomes an increasing attraction!

Even if you live in the smallest accommodation, I hope 'The Shed' shows that you don't have to have a lot of space to have a layout. Admittedly interest might pall after a long period of time, but I must admit that I found it very enjoyable, if not therapeutic, to build and finish the layout in a fairly short time.

The Melbridge Box Company
by Phil Parker

An overall view of 'The Melbridge Box Company' layout by Phil Parker. It says it all! *Mike Wild, courtesy of Hornby Magazine*

Sitting in a Double O Gauge Association annual get-together a few years ago, discussing ways of celebrating the organisation's tenth birthday, someone suggested a layout-building competition. Knowing our members, nothing too ambitious was in order, but gradually the idea was refined to building models in A4-sized box files. Somehow it also ended up that I was going to organise everything.

Those who have worked in an office know box files as things for storing paper, and have probably never taken much notice of their construction. Investigations in a local stationery store showed that not all files are created equal: some are pure cardboard but others have a thin chipboard spine. The latter are a good bet for layout-building purposes and, as the rules allowed for several files to be joined together, £5 later I owned a couple of 'baseboards'.

Inspiration came from Carl Arendt's micro layouts website (www.carendt.us), but didn't give me much help with the nitty gritty. An industrial setting seemed to offer the most possibilities as I could build a small scene apparently within a large factory complex. You don't get much OO track in an A4 space so most of the line had to be off-scene. My files were joined together so one could be scenic and the other the fiddle yard. With a couple of Y-points on the visible section and a separate cassette on the opposite side from the yard, I had a run-round loop and siding. Full-sized plans were drawn up using SMP point templates and the

positions of each component altered a little until the wagons fitted.

Since solenoids underneath the board weren't an option, I decided to use a trick from the old days and use bicycle wheel spokes to operate the points. Brass strip rather than rod is my preferred option as it's easier to solder a pin to it, to go through the tie bar. The brass part from an electrical 'chocolate block' fitted to the end of each rod holds a removable wire handle that protrudes through a hole in the file's spine, allowing its removal when the model is packed up. To give the strip somewhere to run a false bottom of very thin MDF covered the layout base with slots were cut for these and also the track wiring and uncoupling magnets.

The track is SMP code 75 rail soldered to PCB sleepers built as a single piece and glued down with PVA. Even though it's very thin, the chipboard spine took quite some cutting with a piercing saw! Wiring is simple, with feeds at the toe end of each point. Polarity switching is handled by microswitches worked by the point operating rods. A Gaugemaster transformer is used, with a hand held controller plugged into a couple of sockets in the box spine. The 'boards' are joined with small bolts and the electrical supply runs through these. This wasn't the best of ideas as it happens – nice brass ones rather then cheapo DIY store rubbish would have worked better.

Buildings were mocked up with cheap cardboard based on photographs. To get the best from the scene the structures needed to be at angles rather than the more obvious round-the-edge configuration. Some of the early versions were discarded or moved until I produced a scene that looked right. Obviously there were practical things to consider – one building had to have an arch to let the track into the cassette, and another needed to be big enough to cover the sockets and point-operating mechanisms. Another consideration was that the file had to close – it was in the rules – so the buildings either had to be short enough to fit under the lid or be dismantled for storage in the box.

The final versions of most of the buildings were made from Daler board covered with Slaters embossed Plasticard or Wills sheet. They all split at the top of the first floor, which handily coincided with a course of bricks, or at least I made sure it did!

The boiler house at the front is a kit-bashed Ratio model. The chimney splits at a seam line and is guyed in place with thin elastic as used for bead jewellery. The low building at the back is an American model; it is HO, but no one ever notices.

Below: **The Planet diesel shunts the yard at the Melbridge Box Co. Such a small loco is essential on such a small layout, but no one would ever guess from the photo that it is built in a box file.** *Phil Parker*

Ground cover is fine sawdust and covers the majority of the sleepers. Poster paints provide colour. Greenery is either flock powder or Heiki puffer grass, both held on with PVA applied liberally to give slightly overgrown trackwork.

The all-important details came from many places, usually unidentified packets picked up over years of rummaging in boxes at shows and old model shops. Inevitably (for me) there is a VW, and this one is a repainted Husky die-cast model.

Three Parkside wagons and a tiny shunter are all the stock required. The locomotive is a Planet diesel built from a Nonneminstre white metal kit running on a Tenshodo 'Spud'. An 03 diesel would work, or better still an ex-L&Y 'Pug', but an 08 looks much too big. Couplings are Mark 1 Sprat & Winkle, operated by permanent magnets buried below the sleepers.

Building in a box file is great fun and no one can complain that they can't find the space for a layout. It's also a useful way to try different techniques for any future larger model. OK, so there isn't a lot of operating potential, but that doesn't bother me much as I'm more of a builder than operator. Since my 'real' layouts are normally packed away, the Box Company also gives me a small test track that lives in a bookcase.

The Hellingly Hospital Railway
by Phil Parker

When the new asylum built for East Sussex County Council was completed in 1902, the Visiting Committee took the revolutionary step of not only retaining the contractor's railway used in the construction, but electrifying it, creating one of the most unusual railway lines in the country. Intended to bring coal to the hospital generating station, it also had a limited passenger service ferrying patients and visitors from nearby Hellingly station. Throughout its life the line had one locomotive and a tramcar, although the latter fell into disuse when the passenger service ended in 1931. The line itself lasted until 10 March 1959.

I built the model because of the delightful drawing on the front of the book *The Hellingly Hospital Railway* by Peter A. Harding, which aroused my interest in unusual railways. The plan was to build a model that could be transported on the back seat of my classic VW Beetle, which limited the scenic section to 3 feet long and 18 inches wide. While the model was to be as accurate as possible, the nature of the line lent itself to producing a pretty three-dimensional picture. Therefore on the left-hand side the model shows a garden scene that becomes more built up as the eye moves to the right.

The baseboards are 6mm plywood, and the scenic section is accommodated on a single board that features a hinged front to protect the model. The fiddle yards hang on the ends attached by demountable hinges and furniture connecting

blocks. Presentation is diorama-style, so a lighting pelmet is built in, illumination being supplied by a fluorescent tube, giving a bright and even coverage.

All trackwork is scratch-built using SMP rail on copper-clad sleepers with point operation provided by a manual system based on parts used by aero modellers for moving rudders – essentially a plastic wire-in-tube system. At the back of the layout there is a wooden knob on the end of the 'wire', and under the point an operating unit made up from square brass tube is attached, which also incorporates a microswitch to change the frog polarity.

Construction of the overhead proved to be the hardest part of the model. Traction poles were easy to make up from K&S brass tube; while not perfectly accurate, they are more acceptable than any of the commercial offerings. The wire is fine steel – a pig to solder, but better than any of the alternatives tried; copper stretched badly, and nickel worked but if it kinked it couldn't be straightened. A tramway modelling supplier suggested phosphor bronze, but the supplied wire was coated and wouldn't accept solder. The frogs are cast brass from Tramalan after efforts with finer etched-brass versions were too unreliable.

The locomotive featured a trolley pole and this proved to be fundamental to the way the layout developed. My original plan to operate with this loco quickly changed when I discovered how impractical this was. For a start, every time the train reverses, the pole has to be de-wired, rotated and re-wired. Worse, changes in temperature meant simply keeping it running along the wire was a challenge. I needed to find a way around the problem, and the prototype provided a solution. During construction of the line, the contractors had a steam engine. All

Plan of 'The Hellingly Hospital Railway'. 1 Fiddle yards, 2 Hospital buildings, 3 Weighbridge hut, 4 Engine shed

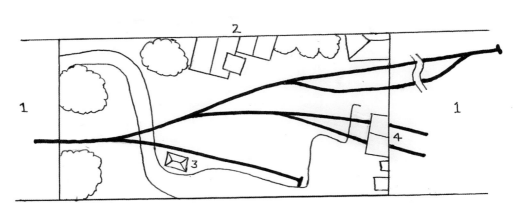

had to do was set the model uring this phase of its life and he electric stock could become l occasional visitor with much lore reliable engines doing the ork. An additional benefit was lat this allowed the running f greater numbers of more lteresting rolling stock than the alf-dozen wagons a week the le boasted in its heyday.

Buildings are Daler board covered with mbossed Plasticard; they are based on photographs f the prototype, especially the engine shed, which ppears in many of the pictures taken by those on ailtours that explored the line in its final days.

The other main structure is the water tower. Both are painted with beige enamel, the brickwork being coloured with pencil crayons rubbed on the surface. This is far easier than doing the same job with paint, although it does leave a slight sheen.

The steam locomotives are from various etched kits. Victorian engines look particularly distinctive with lots of exposed pipework, especially in front of the cab. The electric loco is a Roxey Mouldings kit and the tramcar is scratch-built. The latter took me two goes, as the first attempt in Plasticard didn't work as well as I'd hoped. It wasn't wasted, though, as a little diorama showing it converted into a cricket pavilion, the state in which the prototype spent most of its life, now accompanies the model to exhibitions.

As a construction project, this layout has been a great success. It's been seen at exhibitions up and down the country, including three months in a Birmingham Art Gallery as part of an installation. As a working model it's less effective. The track plan is so simple that operating it for several hours over a weekend isn't a great experience. Fortunately the model does encourage people to talk. We've never been to a show where someone hasn't popped up who knew the line personally,

no matter how far north we are. A combination of being a very 'pretty' picture and a small spotting list of wildlife attached to the display board at the front seems to engage non-enthusiasts more than the 'proper' layouts that surround us.

The other area where the layout falls down is accuracy. When the project started, all the information was contained in a small book. Living 150 miles from the site made a proper visit difficult, not helped by the fact that it was still partly in use as a hospital. On the first trip I made I couldn't get inside the gates! This led to some poor positioning of the buildings; the water tower is behind the engine shed, not beside it as one of the photos appears to show. I have acquired an awful lot of extra information including dozens of previously unpublished photographs. I think this demonstrates the strength of recreating a prototype – the model becomes just part of a greater whole.

Flockburgh
by Phil Parker

Set in the later days of steam, 'Flockburgh' represents the end of a small branch line on the border between England and Scotland. Originally an undistinguished fishing port, the town was developed as a tourist trap intended to rival Blackpool. Sadly the crowds never flocked, so Dr Beeching's axe is hovering. Healthy goods traffic ensures survival for now, and a steady trickle of passengers still uses the service provided.

If this sounds a bit unconvincing, then it is. 'Flockburgh' was built as a test bed for 3mm-scale stock in anticipation of a larger project. After several 4mm layouts, a change was needed to keep up the interest of my father and myself in modelling, and 3mm scale offered the ideal compromise between detail and ease of construction. Thanks to the efforts of the 3mm Society, there are enough kits to allow us to build a layout like this without resorting to scratch-building everything. In fact, it was the availability of etched locomotive kits and plastic wagons that persuaded us that the idea was viable. With nothing other than relatively crude 1960s Triang available ready-to-run, the scale allows modellers who get pleasure from the process of building things to create something that shouldn't

provoke the question 'Is it Bachmann, mister?' every time a locomotive draws into the station.

Despite the drop in scale, most of the construction techniques are those developed for the OO layout. The baseboards are 9mm plywood cut to size by local traditional hardware store, and are joined with loose pin hinges bought from a DIY shop. In fact there are only four bolts in the whole layout, and these hold the lighting poles to the back of the legs. Years of clambering under models at exhibitions searching for lost nuts has convinced us to design them out wherever possible.

The fiddle yard is a traverser carried on runners intended for filing cabinets but available separately; the overall length of the layout had to be constrained to 9 feet so it could be set up in our living room, so a traditional fan of points wasn't an option. Locomotives and rolling stock are mainly kit-built from etched brass, plastic and white metal kits. Couplings are Sprat & Winkle Mark 1s operated by permanent magnets.

Trackwork is scratch-built from code 60 rail and copper-clad sleepers. All points are operated by Peco point motors. We had chosen to use the finest rack gauge supported by the Society – 14.2mm – and this initially seemed sensible as with kit-built olling stock it ought to be no harder than the more raditional 12mm gauge. Sadly, this was not to be – he finer standards are much more demanding than he rough-and-ready OO worker, like me, is used o. We spent many frustrating hours running stock

around and wondering why it fell off – in the early stages it was impossible to know whether the fault was in the loco or the track. Eventually, and after a lot of gauge widening, running became acceptable.

With experience, I now have a 'recipe' for successful models. All locomotives with six wheels must be compensated. Diesels utilise Sharman OO

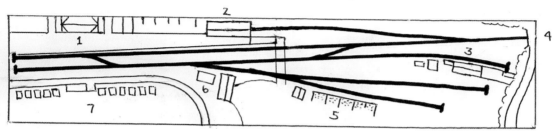

Above: **Plan of 'Flockburgh. 1 Station, 2 Engine shed, 3 Goods shed, 4 To fiddle yard, 5 Coal yard, 6 Water tank, 7 Beach**

elow: **The coal staithes are in the foreground with the 0-6-0 tank loco shunting behind and a loco about to go on shed. I particularly like the Flockburgh Fisheries poster on the retaining wall.** *Phil Parker*

wheels suitably regauged as the slightly over-scale flanges are hidden away. Talking to other modellers, I'm not the only one employing this subterfuge!

Buildings make use of Daler board and Plasticard and are based on photographs taken of prototypes from around the country. The station and goods shed are based on prototypes from the Cawood, Wistow & Selby Light Railway as we had the plans. While not really appropriate for a Scottish station, the attitude is very much 'It's our train set, we'll do what we want.'

After exhibiting the model a few times, no less a personage than the late Cyril Freezer suggested that the display would be improved if we had a small scenic section beyond the end of the station. This would explain why the line finishes where it does – in real life this was simply because it had reached the end of the baseboard, but we had to admit that it did look a bit odd. A short board was made up and deliberations started as to exactly what should go there. The board even appeared at an exhibition with a sign on it requesting suggestions. In the end a small harbour entrance loosely based on Laxey, Isle of Man, was constructed. The effect on the layout

is considerable. The end now 'makes sense' as the railway company couldn't go any further except by demolishing the chapel and filling in the harbour. All of this is based on prototype arrangements, so looks acceptable.

As a test bed 'Flockburgh' has worked very well. We now own quite a bit of rolling stock that could be transferred to a future layout and be relied on. This makes track-building easier and any problems will be here rather than with the locomotives. So far nothing has come of these plans as the layout is proving popular with exhibition managers, something that can only be attributed to the unusual scale. If built in OO, nearly everything could be bought off the shelf and would be a lot less interesting to the public.

For modellers with limited space, 3mm scale has a great deal to commend it. In OO our layout would need to be at least 15 feet long and therefore wouldn't fit in the house. Because everything has to be built, the pleasure of construction extends over a longer period. Thanks to the support of the 3mm Society, though, you have access to plenty to resources to help, so it's not too painful.

Below: **Another shunting move at Flockburgh. Note the supported timber in the background, often seen but not often modelled.** *Phil Parker*

Maesog, Kinwardine Wharf and Winter Overcotes by Charles Insley

These layouts were built over a 10-year period between 1997 and 2007 and were all built in very different circumstances from my layouts described in *Layouts for Limited Spaces*. All three are different in their own ways, but there are also common features that are worth bringing out.

First, all are narrow gauge in 4mm scale, generally known as 009. This has been a feature of my modelling now for nearly 30 years, and I do not suppose it is going to change now! This scale/gauge combination has both advantages and disadvantages to the modeller. Most narrow-gauge lines, especially those in the UK, were very idiosyncratic affairs, an attractive feature if one wants to get away from the world of ready-to-run uniformity. Narrow gauge is also ripe for a freelance approach, although good freelance modelling is far harder than prototype; after all, for the prototype it is all there for you, either in photograph or in real life. The freelance modeller has to build a model that is convincing and believable, without the advantages of the prototype. The downside when modelling UK narrow gauge is the absence of ready-to-run equipment. There are, however, plenty of kits, for both locomotives and rolling stock, readily available. These range from the simple and relatively cheap white metal kits that simply drop on top of a ready-to-run N-gauge mechanism, to etched brass kits costing well over £100. The 009 Society also has an excellent second-hand sales operation from which it is possible to purchase made-up and painted kit-built locomotives and rolling stock

My layouts have also got a lot smaller. My earlier layouts, in particular 'Glastraeth' (009) and 'Caher Patrick' (TTn3) were relatively large – 8 and 7 feet long respectively. This was possible because they were built and stored in the parental home. However, by the time 'Caher Patrick' was finished (1996) I had moved away from home and needed a layout that could be kept in a small flat. Since then, although I have purchased a house, I have also acquired a family – two small children and an immensely understanding wife. In particular, the fact that railway exhibitions tend to be family affairs means that the layout is fighting for space in the car with stuff for three or four people. The result is that the three layouts described here are all less than 4ft 6in long.

However, I do not view the smaller size of my recent layouts as a constraint or disadvantage. The fact that I model narrow gauge makes small layouts more plausible. The key is to strike a good balance between operational interest and cramming the layout with too much track. The other technique I use is to design the scenery so that it creates the impression that there is much more than there is; one can do this with mirrors, but also by breaking the layout down into a series of scenes that add up to more than the whole. I remember, after 'Caher Patrick' was featured in a high-profile modelling magazine, people commenting at shows that the layout, in real life, was smaller than it appeared in the magazine. Part of this was skilful photography, part the way the layout had been designed.

The three layouts described here are all exhibition layouts, and this means a number of things. First, they must be well presented. One can read much in the model railway press about the presentation of layouts, and one sees at model railway shows layouts that are presented in highly theatrical ways, with 'proscenium arches' and pelmet lighting. The presentation of my layouts is pretty simple compared to what could be done; the key is to ensure that the layout is adequately lit and at a reasonable height – I find that around 40 inches works well, neither so low that unless one kneels down one gets an unrealistic 'helicopter eye' view of the layout, nor so high that smaller visitors or those in wheelchairs are completely excluded. That said, any height other than eye level for an adult will involve some sort of compromise.

Second, the layout needs to be durable, capable of withstanding being put up and the wear and tear of being slung in and out of cars, but at the same time light and portable enough for one person to carry and, if necessary, set up. My carpentry and woodworking skills are pretty basic, so complex baseboards are not necessarily my cup of tea. Like all modellers, I have evolved a method that suits and works for me. If you are better at woodwork than I am, by all means go for the various sorts of open-frame baseboards. What I do, though, is construct a traditional planed timber frame, on top of which I put the boards. However, rather than using the heavy Sundeala beloved of earlier generations of modellers, I use lightweight materials such as balsa or foam-cored artists' mounting board. Both are pretty robust, if braced adequately, and can be carved and shaped; it is also easy to glue down track and carve around for things like point control wiring. What I find is that my layouts are easy to move around, but are capable of standing up to quite some abuse – indeed, the oldest layout, 'Maesog', is still going strong at 12 years old, despite having been transported on trains in its early years before I mastered the art of driving.

Third, the layout needs to be easy to set up, either at home or at exhibitions. 'Maesog', the oldest, is also the easiest to set up, since it consists of just one board. It travels in a box structure that protects it and upon which it sits at exhibitions, both the box and the layout sitting on a table. Mention of tables bring us on to one of the more vexed questions surrounding exhibitions layouts: whether to have self-contained legs or not. Of the three layouts here, two ('Maesog' and 'Kinwardine Wharf') sit on tables, while the third, 'Winter Overcotes', has its own legs. Generally speaking, I find that not having to take legs or some other support structure with you saves space in the car, but leaves you at the mercy of wobbly or otherwise inadequate tables at railway shows. I also find that the average table is too low for the layout to be at a satisfactory height. One way around this, I have found, is to do as I have done with 'Maesog', where the layout sits on top of its own storage and transport box, on top of a table or tables. I have also used a variation on this for 'Kinwardine Wharf', where the layout sits on two cheap collapsible packing crates of the sort readily available from DIY stores. One of these crates is used to transport things like the stock and controllers, while the other is carried flat. Both are used, upside down on a table, to support the layout. 'Winter Overcotes' is the departure from this, since it has its own trestles (modified Homebase plastic saw-horses); this was done because of the L-shaped configuration of the baseboards. In fact, my current layout project, a French narrow gauge layout in HOe, is also L-shaped and uses the same trestles as 'Winter Overcotes'.

Another common feature of the layouts, and a departure from my previous efforts, is that they are all end-to-end in format. In part this was driven by the reduction in the size of layouts I was building – squeezing an oval of track onto a board 4 feet by 1 foot would have been a challenge. Also, though, I was getting tired of the compromises necessary to squeeze an oval onto even a 2-foot-wide board; to my mind, it looks unrealistic and creates unnecessary challenges for smooth running. The downside is that one loses the ability to just let the trains run round and chase their tails, but to be absolutely honest this is not something I have missed, and anyway it is far outweighed by not having my stock derail on too-tight curves. Another upshot of this is the need to think more about the off-scene area, ie the fiddle yard. On an oval, this tends to be the rear of the layout. On an end-to-end layout, especially a narrow one, this is not really an option and generally most people tack a fiddle yard onto the end of the layout. The other problem is that a fiddle yard capable of storing a useful number of trains can be quite large, so the risk is that one ends up with quite a lot of what we might call 'dead space'.

There are, of course, many ways around this, but the particular method I have seized on is the use of cassettes to store trains, which can then be slotted into the layout as necessary. I am a complete convert to this system, since you can more or less have as many cassettes as you want, but they take up very little space on the layout. They also reduce the need for operators to handle the stock (there is no need, for instance, to pick the loco up and move it to the other end of the train) since the whole cassette can be turned around. My earlier cassettes were made of plastic and PVC angle, but I have since gone over to using aluminium angle on a plastic base; the advantage of this is that the aluminium can also be used as the track!

Having described some of the general points and features common to all three layouts, it is time to meet them individually.

'Maesog'

A view of Maesog station building and some superb rolling stock. *M. Thornton*

This was built in 1997-98. It was actually purchased from Paul Towers, since Paul's desire to sell it coincided with my need for a very small and very portable layout. I have retained Paul's trackwork, although rewired to suit my own needs, but the scenery and structures have been added from scratch. The aim of 'Maesog' was to capture the flavour of the Welsh narrow gauge without being a model of any one particular line, although at the time I was building it I was heavily into the Corris Railway. The track plan is simple but effective - a passing loop with a couple of sidings. There is enough operational interest in the layout to stop one from getting completely bored over a two-day show. If I had built the layout completely from scratch, the one thing I may have done differently would have been to place the exit to the fiddle yard towards the back of the layout (as on 'Kinwardine Wharf') and would have some sort of kick-back siding in front of it to disguise it; this would have avoided the 9 or 10 inches of dead space at the front of the layout. Since the layout is small, there are only two buildings: a Wills 'tin chapel' and a modified and repainted Peco station building. The rest of the scenery consists of trees and shrubs made by my mother, who has made greenery for all of my layouts over the last twenty years!

Plan of 'Maesog'. 1 Station building, 2 'Tin chapel', 3 Goods platform, 4 Footbridge, 5 Cassettes, 6 Controller

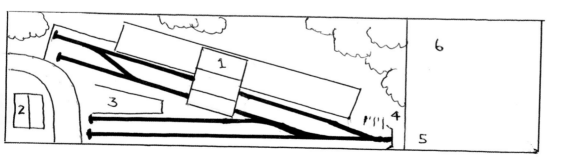

Above: **A close-up of a loco running round at Maesog.** M. *Thornton*

'Kinwardine Wharf'

Canals have always interested me – partly because today a narrow boat is a very enjoyable way to travel, but also because their history was often tied up with, but also distinct from, the railways. I had decided, therefore, that my next layout would have a canal on it. Canals often appear on model railway layouts, generally as space-fillers; however I wanted my canal not to be a 'scenic extra', but key feature of the layout, with a lock and a wharf. Thus was born 'Kinwardine Wharf', a layout set somewhere on the Shropshire Union Canal (and

Plan of 'Kinwardine Wharf'. 1 Fiddle yard, 2 Warehouse, Canal, 4 Half-relief shops, 5 Station building, 6 Lock

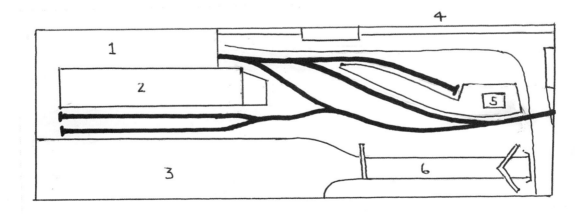

he first layout I have ever built not set in Wales
or Ireland!). The basic concept here was that the
narrow-gauge railway had to squeeze itself in by
the canal, which had been built in the 1820s. The
layout itself is dominated by a
large warehouse complex, based
on the bonded warehouse in
Stourbridge, on the Birmingham
Canal Navigations.

The layout was built between
2002 and 2004 and follows the
format discussed above; a simple
frame of planed timber, topped
in this case with foamboard.
The datum level is the canal,
with further layers of foamboard
to form dry land. The overall
structure is very light and pretty
durable – it has survived five
years of exhibiting so far with
no ill effects. The track plan
differs from 'Maesog', in that
the fiddle yard/cassette storage is

Above: **A lovely view of the wharf, which, together with the
boat, really adds to the scene.** M. *Thornton*

Below: **An overall view of 'Kinwardine Wharf' – again, note
the detail.** M. *Thornton*

at the back of the layout, behind the warehouse, while there is a long kick-back siding that runs in front of the warehouse along the edge of the canal. 'Kinwardine Wharf' is also set in a town, so many more buildings were required; these are a mixture of scratch-built (by my father) and kit-built, mainly from the excellent (although not cheap) Langley Masterbuild range. The canal itself was painted in a number of shades of mucky greeny brown, before receiving several coats of yacht varnish. The overall result is pretty effective and the varnish seems to have had no ill effects on the foamboard.

The canal is also well stocked with boats, which are mostly kit-built, although a Hornby 'Skaledale' steamer has made an appearance, suitably detailed and repainted. In some respects, the boats were the most enjoyable part of building the layout, since I was determined to try and make the boats accurate, especially in terms of the liveries. This is a complex subject, as complex (if not more so) than railway liveries; the boats on the layout all belong to individuals or companies active on the Shropshire Union in the late 1920s.

'Winter Overcotes'

The third layout of the trio is a joint project between myself and my wife; the overall concept and inspiration is hers. It is set in the fictional county of Barsetshire and was inspired by the novels of Angela Thirkell, who set a large number of stories there between the 1920s and the 1950s. The other departure here is that the railway modelled is actually a narrow-gauge branch of the Great Western Railway/BR Western Region, rather like the Vale of Rheidol or the Welshpool & Llanfair. The layout is also set just after nationalisation, so a lot of the stock is still in worn GWR livery, while some is in BR livery. The model represents a junction between the narrow gauge East Barsetshire Light Railway and the main line to Barchester; there is an exchange siding between the standard and narrow gauges, while the viewer of the layout stands where the standard gauge main line would be.

Construction is similar to the previous layouts, with a simple timber frame topped with 3/8-inch balsa. The two boards are the same size as those of 'Kinwardine Wharf' (30 by 20 inches); however, here they are at right-

angles to each other, and the narrow-gauge line disappears off to the 'rest of the world', or at least Barsetshire, around a sweeping curve. This L-shaped configuration means that the layout has its own legs, rather than sitting on tables; these are modified sawhorses from Homebase.

The buildings were built by my wife (station building, signal box, engine shed) and my father (row of terraced houses); once again the greenery was supplied by my mother. The stock is a mixture of kit-built and modified ancient ready-to-run Eggerbahn HOe from the early 1970s. One advantage I have discovered of setting the layout in the early 1950s is the recent explosion of die-cast cars in 4mm scale from that period; this means

Plan of 'Winter Overcotes'.
1 Turntable, 2 Narrow-gauge station, 3 Signal box, 4 Level crossing, 5 Railwaymen's terrace, 6 Engine shed, 7 Standard-gauge exchange siding, 8 Standard-gauge platform, 9 Fiddle yard, 10 Allotments

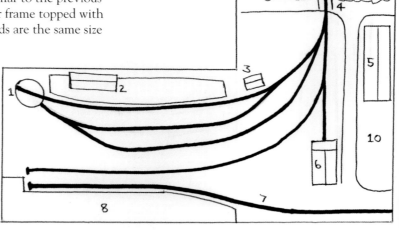

Above: **A view of 'Winter Overcotes' looking towards the buffers.** M. *Thornton*

Below: **Looking in the other direction, it all looks very real!** M. *Thornton*

...at I can populate the layout with Series 1 Morris
...inors, Morris Eights, Austin taxis and the like. It
... tempting to cover the layout in these very nice
...rs, but that temptation needs
...o be resisted; cars were still
...ot that common in the early
...950s.

These layouts are all still
...oing strong as exhibition
...ayouts; their small size means
...hat they are easy to transport
...nd set up, while careful design
...leans that they are fun to
...perate. If you are building an
...xhibition layout, you need
...o remember that it needs to
...e not just enjoyable to play
...rains with for an hour in the
...vening, but to operate over

a day or two days. Get the design right and that
should not be a problem!

Tryweryn
A North Wales freight-only terminus
by Martin Jones

The inspiration for 'Tryweryn' came from a variety of different sources – discovering the remains of the former GWR Bala to Blaenau Ffestiniog branch, a planning article by Neil Rushby in *British Railway Modelling* with a similar idea in the same area I had in mind, and the timely availability of several items from the likes of Bachmann and Parkside Dundas, together with one further factor, a decision to model in EM gauge.

An invitation to operate a layout at a York show sowed the seeds of the idea. At the same show I came across a number of EM-gauge layouts, which subsequently led me to join the EM Gauge Society, a decision that I have never regretted, as a visit to any of the 'Expo' events will explain – a friendly and relaxed atmosphere.

Some happy teenage camping holidays were spent close to the Cambrian Coast line and a birthday treat was an excursion to Barmouth or Tywyn complete with a fish'n'chip supper. Thus the prototype had to be based in North Wales and set in the diesel era, due to the ease of conversion from OO, even thought my main modelling interest at the time was the London Midland Region in the late 1950s.

This in turn led to scrutiny of the Conwy Valley line and the subsequent connection of the ex-LNWR/LMS and GWR lines to facilitate the transfer of nuclear fuel from Trawsfynydd Power Station.

The Bala & Ffestiniog Railway built by the GWR and initially dual-gauged as far as Llan Ffestiniog was designed to tap into the slate wealth of the Vale of Ffestiniog and opened throughout in 1882 from Bala Junction to Blaenau Ffestiniog, a distance of some 25 miles through some of the most rugged scenery in North Wales. Unusually for the GWR, however, it never capitalised on the scenic delights of its route into southern Snowdonia and the line led a fairly uneventful existence until the late 1950s when Liverpool Corporation found its water supply insufficient to meet future needs.

This required the Tryweryn valley to be flooded to meet the ever-increasing demand. Part of the route would be affected by the new reservoir and, despite plans and finance to re-route the line, complete closure was decided upon. However, it seemed that there was a future for the northern end of the line, to facilitate the construction of Trawsfynydd Power Station. Connected in 1964, this still exists today, albeit disused. To justify the layout's existence, therefore, my presumption was that a freight railhead was retained east of Trawsfynydd serving the Tryweryn valley.

The foundations for 'Tryweryn', a first excursion into finescale modelling, were built from 9mm plywood, the overall dimensions being 8 feet by 1ft 9in, split into two for ease of transportation. Trackwork is SMP laid on ⅛-inch cork with manual point control using DPDT slider switches and brass rodding – simple, robust and cost-effective.

Expanded polystyrene sheets were used to build up the scenic contours, then covered with plaster shell, painted, and Woodland Scenics flock and foliage added. The infrastructure was then tackled with Wills Scenic Series kits, together with selected items from the Ten Commandments range and a Ratio coal hopper modified to represent a gravel hopper fed from an offstage quarry.

Ten Bachmann Type 2s of Classes 24 and 25 represent the motive power, although other types are also available, being easy to convert to 18.2mm gauge, and are numbered to represent locally based examples, all weathered appropriately and fitted

Plan of 'Tryweryn'. 1 Dock, 2 Coal staithe, 3 Fiddle yard, 4 Stone hopper

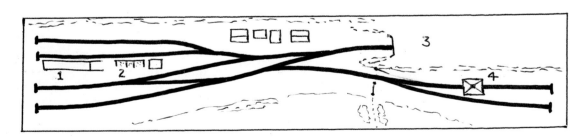

with bufferbeam details and Smiths couplings. Both green and Rail Blue examples are employed, portraying various periods from 1966 to the mid-1980s.

Some 100-plus items of rolling stock are available, far too much for such a small layout, but I enjoy building rolling stock and modifying ready-to-run examples from the excellent Parkside Dundas and Bachmann ranges. All the stock is weathered to some degree as rolling stock is my forte, and all are fitted with Alan Gibson or Romford wheels and Smiths couplings to represent the common-user types found at the time.

I find one of the most satisfying aspects of the hobby is to exhibit the layout at shows: I aim to keep operation varied, with a track plan designed for shunting, and try to maintain a variety of services, including engineer's specials in addition to normal freight services, using the appropriate stock relevant to the period depicted.

Above: **A view showing almost the whole of 'Tryweryn'.**
Steve Flint, *courtesy of Railway Modeller*

Thanks are due to my wife Tracey for her forbearance and patience, Peter Midwinter, Neil Rushby, Neil Ripley and lastly the EMGS for improving my standards. As to the future, the next EM layout will be 'Kinmundy', set in the Buchan area of North East Scotland on ex-GNSR lines in the early blue diesel era, and plans are close to fruition, with suitable stock already acquired, built and modified.

Below: **A very atmospheric picture of a rather overgrown yard.**
The scenic detail on this layout is excellent. Steve Flint, *courtesy of Railway Modeller*

Nuffin, Mointeach na hInse Lia, Random, Keighpatt Bay and Overkill by Richard Insley

When Richard Insley began building model railways back in the early 1970s he set himself a list of targets:

- Scenery to be as realistic as possible for the location
- Enough dioramas to occupy the public when the trains do not run
- Humorous names for buildings and firms
- Figures in realistic poses and positions (they need not be named)
- Building and exhibiting must be fun

You will notice that size or transportation do not feature in that list. They do now. By the last decade of the last century, Richard had settled on a layout size not exceeding 8 feet by 2ft 6in, an exhibition footprint of 10 feet by 6 feet. A sectional, folding six-legged table of 10 by 2 feet is the base of all new layouts, and all those described here conform to that footprint.

'Nuffin' (N)

Having built and exhibited 'Clemens Landing' (featured in *Layouts for Limited Spaces*), set in the USA in the 1850s, Richard decided to build an urban layout set in the USA in the 1950s. Lessons learned building 'Clemens Landing' were used again, and some extra ones. Size was determined by the need to fit the layout into the back of an Astra, and weight by the need to hang it on a wall.

Below: **Richard Insley's sketch of 'Nuffin'.**

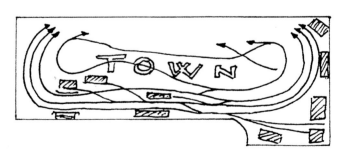

The baseboards (and all subsequent baseboards are made from timber and plywood held together with white glue and screws, braced underneath with timber drilled for wiring. Weight is made as light as possible by using 'polyboard', a sandwich of foam between two layers of thin card that artists and others use for display mounting. It is lightweight as well as strong and forms the core of all Richard's buildings. The other material is expanded polystyrene, not the stuff that flakes all over the place like static confetti, sticks to hands and other exposed flesh, and keeps on appearing five vacuumings later, but the stuff that comes in electrical goods packaging and generally gets thrown away as the latest gismo is hurriedly unwrapped. We all work somewhere where last week's computer system is being updated, and when unpacked, out the back by the bins where the smokers huddle, will be a layout's worth of scenery base.

As can be seen from the track plan, the layout is a series of loops with sidings. The two outer loops are the main lines and are the ones with sidings, hence the shunting. The third inner line is an 'inter-urban' railroad, with scratch-built overhead wires, while the innermost line is a trolley (tram) line. The fiddle yard at the back is seven lines wide, the biggest fiddle yard Richard has ever used. The track and points are Peco 'N' laid on cork and ballasted in the usual manner. Since the period is the transition from steam to diesel, steam runs in the morning of an exhibition, diesel in the afternoon. What is different about the layout is that the town is set in no one location, its geographical place changing from day to day at an exhibition, thus allowing Richard to run a variety of stock, some specially modified and painted.

Most of the buildings are kits or modified kits, all of plastic. Some are DPM modular kits while others are heavily modified structures. All foreground buildings have internal fittings and lighting. The scenery, where it can be seen, is grass mat and scatter. Road vehicles come from the range produced to advertise the film *Dick Tracy* and are hard to find today. Figures are Preiser (unpainted are cheaper), surgically modified and repainted.

Above: **A superb shot of 'Nuffin' showing the scenic detail.**
Denyse Insley

Below: **This photograph shows the importance of the buildings, figures and vehicles to the overall scene, bringing the layout to life.** *Denyse Insley*

'Mointeach na hInse Lia' (009)

A family trip to Ireland found the Insleys very much taken with the narrow-gauge peat railways of the Bord na Mona. From this sprang a layout. Unlike all the others, this one is only 4 feet long and, with little rolling stock, has the advantage of being able to be set up in 10 to 20 minutes, depending on how far it has to be carried. As can be seen from the track plan, it is a loop with a

Richard's wife scope for her tree-making, several trees native to central Ireland being featured.

This part of the layout has scratch-built models of the various eclectic machines used by the Bord na Mona. The locomotives are Bachmann N-gauge Plymouths with scratch-built bodies to resemble the 'Wagonmasters' used by the Bord na Mona. Loaded wagons go out and empty wagons return, the change-over taking place on a 6-inch-long fiddle yard hidden behind some trees.

figure of eight dividing the board into two. One side has the natural bog while the other side has the bog being worked. The track is Peco 009 track with N-gauge points laid on cork. With a loop and figure of eight the wiring is interesting.

The natural bog has on it various species of wildlife and birds. For the worked bog, Richard experimented with fur fabric, as used to make teddy bears and other soft toys. Dyed green unevenly and brushed, it provides the springy base for the bog. It is covered with actual peat secured with diluted white glue. This layout, unlike 'Nuffin', gave

Above: **A view showing the loading of the peat. Note the swans in the background.** *Len Weal, courtesy of Railway Modeller*

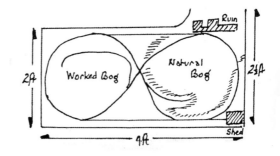

'Random' (N, Nn3)

This layout was built mainly to show off the trees made by Richard's wife, there being more than 100 in the 8-by-3-foot space. The layout is a return to the USA and is set in the Catskill Mountains in the autumn of 1929. This means bright yellow, red and orange trees. On this layout Richard experimented with Nn3 using Z-gauge track with scratch-built bodies on Z mechanisms. This is an experiment he is unlikely to repeat. The track plan may look like a double oval but is operated as two separate lines, each entering from the two ends and each being a separate railroad company. The scenery is 'polyboard' or polystyrene covered with grass mat and various flocks. All the buildings are scratch-built, as are many of the locomotives and railcars. The telegraph wires are elastic thread, a successful experiment tried out first on this layout. Also included is a lake at the front with various scratch-built boats.

Random (N, Nn3).

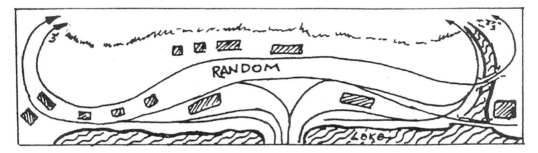

Below: **The trees made by Denyse Insley are a big feature in this photo.** *Denyse Insley*

Above: **A short train passes through the scenery. For me, this gives the right impression – that the rest of the scene was** there first and the railway is part of it, rather than being a layout to which scenery has been added. *Denyse Insley*

'Keighpatt Bay' (HO)

As an historian Richard has always been interested in the very early days of railroads, especially in the USA. Since there is no N-gauge stock of this period – 1838 – Richard was forced to move to HO gauge. This made him consider using an extended fiddle yard with cassettes set at right angles to the layout. Electrical contact is made with brass strips that rest on copper-clad insulated sleepers on the cassettes, which are made from plastic L-shaped lengths.

The track plan has two distinct lines with no connection, one lower than the other. The track is Peco code 75 HO track with

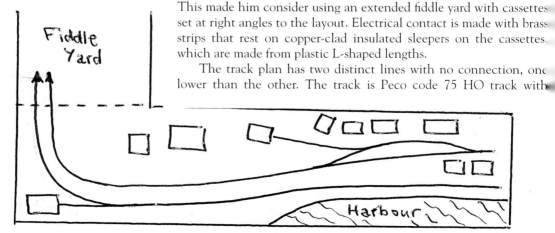

Right: **This photograph says it all! A very effective layout with very effective scenery, and an unusual loco passing through with its train.** *Steve Flint, courtesy of Railway Modeller*

alternate sleepers removed so as to resemble the 4ft 9in track of the original Camden & Amboy Railroad laid on stone blocks. Since laying two stone blocks per sleeper could lead to madness, only a few are laid, the ballast being taken up to the top of the sleepers. As with all his layouts, Richard operates his points using wire-in-tube. It may lack the sophistication of point motors and DCC but it is a cheap, reliable and easy to repair.

The scenery is grass mat, various flocks, Silflor and static grass, and his wife's trees, all in spring growth and blossom. A ploughed field is corrugated cardboard covered with brown paint mixed with N-gauge ballast. Since there are no kits of New Jersey buildings of 1838, all had to be scratch-built using plastic and, for the first time since the 1950s, strip wood. All the buildings are based on those in New Jersey or Pennsylvania of the period and have interiors and lighting. The Delaware River at the front is made of a plastic sheet with preformed ripples laid a quarter of an inch above a dark painted base. On this river is a scratch-built New England schooner and a heavily modified Russian kit of a paddle steamer of the 1830s.

The locomotives are all Bachmann and are modified or re-motored and in one case scratch-built. Two vertical-boilered affairs are built on the Bachmann 'Gandy Dancer'. The passenger stock is mainly Bachmann or Keyser, all repainted, while the freight stock is all scratch-built. People were not a problem, since Preiser and Merten produce figures of the period, but they were an expense. Many are modified and repainted, female dresses being augmented with strips of lead. Vehicles are either Preiser or scratch-built. The beauty of modelling a period like 1838 is that there are very few experts out there to contradict the models.

'Overkill' (On30)

A chance purchase of a Bachmann On30 locomotive led, in time, to the construction of this layout. The 8-foot length is not a problem even in O scale since the narrow gauge allows tight curves and short trains. As with 'Keighpatt Bay', this layout has a fiddle yard and cassettes. As can be seen from the track plan, it is simple, laid with Peco 0-16.5 track and very few points; the wire-and-tube method allows Richard to have working target switch-stands. After much research Richard settled on the Catskill & Tannersville Railroad, the period being 1906. Most of the scenery is dyed fur fabric, combed to produce tall grass, some Silflor and some flocks. Trees and flowers are, naturally, made by Richard's wife.

The two buildings, the engine shed and depot, are scratch-built in strip wood and scale lumber, stained with Indian ink and marker pens. Both

buildings have fully detailed interiors and lighting. Richard discovered that the bigger the scale the more detail has to be included, such as screw heads. The people who are holidaying on the layout are Aiden Campbell white metal figures requiring skirts fashioned from the lead from the tops of wine bottles, and real feathers in their hats. Suitcases are made of plastic, the crates of wood.

All of the layouts described here have been enjoyable to build and operate and each has given Richard the chance to try out new ideas, new scales and new techniques, a process that is continuing.

Top: A train entering Overkill station. Note the wooden platform and walkway on the track, and the 'period' figures. M. Thornton

Above: A superb close-up of an engine on shed. M. Thornton

Right: Sketch of 'Overkill'

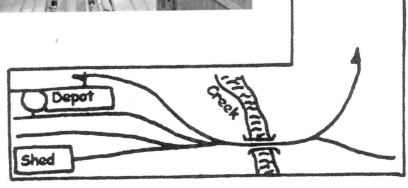

BIBLIOGRAPHY

Many well-known modellers have written books on the subject that are full of ideas. The following list is by no means exhaustive, but rather is simply a list of books that I have bought in the past because I have found them useful.

Arendt, Carl *Creating Micro Layouts*
    Small Layout Scrapbook
Booth, Trevor *Baseboard Basics and Making Tracks* (Silver Link Publishing)
    Creating the Landscape (Silver Link Publishing)
Danny, Peter *Buckingham Branch*, Books 1 and 2 (Wild Swan)
Flint, Lunn, Ripley, Gibbons and Barnard *Model Railway Planning and Design* (Santona Publications)
Freezer, C. J. *Model Railway Design Manual* (Patrick Stephens Limited)
    Model Railway Operation (Patrick Stephens Limited)
Futers, Ian *Modelling Scotland's Railways* (Santona Publications)
Gravett, Gordon *7mm Modelling* Parts 1 and 2 (Wild Swan)
Kazer, Peter *Narrow Gauge Railway Modelling* (Wild Swan)
Lunn, Paul *Building Micro Layouts* (Santona Publications)
Marriott, Peter *Model Railways The Easy Way* (BRM Books)
Model Railroading in Small Spaces (Kalmbach Publishing)
Norman, Barry *Designing a Layout* (Wild Swan)
Rice, Iain *Designs for Urban Layouts* (Atlantic)
    Light Railway Layout Design (Wild Swan)
    Railway Modelling the Realistic Way (Haynes Publishing)
    Small, Smart and Practical Track Plans (Model Railroader)
Simmons, Norman *Railway Modelling* (Patrick Stephens Limited)
Various *Small Layouts* Volumes 1 and 2 (Gauge O Guild)

In addition, there are of course the many books published about prototype railways, which are far too numerous to mention, and, in any case, will depend totally on your favourites!

THE SILVER LINK LIBRARY OF RAILWAY MODELLING

The Silver Link Library of Railway Modelling is a growing range of books designed to build into a comprehensive range for modellers at all stages and skill levels of the hobby.

BASEBOARD BASICS AND MAKING TRACKS
Planning * Baseboard construction * Track laying * Wiring
978 1 85794 006 0 Paperback £15.99

CREATING THE SCENIC LANDSCAPE
Stations and buildings * Fields and trees, roads and rivers *
Construction techniques * Painting and detailing
978 1 85794 023 7 Paperback £15.99

LOCOMOTIVE AND ROLLING-STOCK CONSTRUCTION
Choosing suitable stock * Building kits * Painting and detailing *
Realistic operation
978 1 85794 038 1 Paperback £14.99

LAYOUTS FOR LIMITED SPACES
Practical solutions for the space-starved modeller
978 1 85794 055 8 Paperback £16.99

MODEL RAILWAY LOCOMOTIVE BUILDING
ON THE CHEAP!
Volume 1
978 1 85794 289 7 Paperback RPND

MODEL RAILWAY LOCOMOTIVE BUILDING
ON THE CHEAP!
Volume 2
978 1 85794 312 2 Paperback £17.99

SIMPLE MODEL
RAILWAY LAYOUTS
Big ideas for small spaces
978 1 85794 226 2 Paperback £17.99

THE NEWCOMERS' GUIDE TO MODEL RAILWAYS
A step-by-step guide to the complete model railway

Brian Lambert

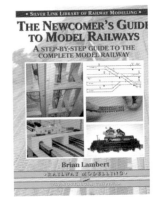

Although Brian Lambert's interests are mainly in the UK OO gauge, this comprehensive book is written to be of assistance to all modellers, no matter what the chosen scale or gauge. Moreover, not only will it guide the beginner to the hobby, it will also aid anyone who has already started to build a model railway. Page by page modellers will be able to gain more information and explore new techniques, from the basics of construction and track-laying to the intricacies of up-to-the-minute Digital Command Control, allowing them to achieve the true goal of the hobby – to build and operate a true model railway, rather than just run a train set.
Sections include:

- Selecting a suitable scale and gauge
- Finding a home for the railway
- Building the baseboard
- Laying the track
- Constructing the landscape
- Electrics and control
- Point operation
- Panels, indications and lighting
- Digital Command Control
- Maintenance and tools

978 1 85794 329 0   Paperback   £17.99

CREATIVE SCENIC MODELLING
A practical approach to model railway landscaping

John Parkinson

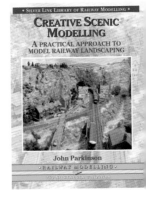

John Parkinson is a self-confessed 'scenery nut'. While for many people the tracks and trains are the most important element of a model railway layout, John revels in creating the scenic environment, which is complemented by the trains running through it. With all his layouts, his aim is to make a scene that gels, that looks like a composite whole, and has atmosphere. He is quick to stress that his is not the only, or necessarily the best, way to approach scenic modelling. He demonstrates that advanced, difficult-to-obtain skills are not needed – just practice and an urge to be creative, to develop a three-dimensional representation of a particular scene, particularly in the smaller scales, where layouts can be more easily and quickly completed. In his personal, informal narrative, he describes how he has developed his modelling skills, and shares the techniques he has used for almost 30 years for his many popular exhibition layouts. Covering natural terrain, foliage, water, buildings, bridges, tunnels and the like to detailing and finishing touches, this book will inspire and instruct in equal measure.
After a career in teaching, John Parkinson moved with his family to Snowdonia, where they fostered handicapped children, before retiring to Blaenau Ffestiniog. A keen railway modeller for many years, he particularly enjoys encouraging younger people to take up the hobby and develop their skills.

978 1 85794 352 8   Paperback   £17.99